Atsugi Assassins

H.E. Jensen

ISBN 0-7414-4077-6

Published by:

INFINITY
PUBLISHING.COM

1094 New DeHaven Street, Suite 100
West Conshohocken, PA 19428-2713
Info@buybooksontheweb.com
www.buybooksontheweb.com
Toll-free (877) BUY BOOK
Local Phone (610) 941-9999
Fax (610) 941-9959

Printed in the United States of America

Printed on Recycled Paper

Published March 2008

Acknowledgments

I want to express gratitude to my daughters, Tracy Jensen and Jill Miller, for their informational feedback, computer assistance, the many times they helped me with my word processing program, and for contributing many hours of editing to develop this book into an understandable read.

I want to give special thanks to my friend Osamu Miyata from Ichinomiya Aichi, Japan, who assisted me with the design of this book's cover. A student at the University of Wisconsin-La Crosse, Osamu translated the words Atsugi Assassins into Chinese Kanji characters.

Special Thanks

To my daughters Tracy and Jill,
who never lost faith in me, and with their encouragement
kept me working on this project.

Table of Contents

Introduction

I have put off completion of this book for a number of years and for a number of reasons. One cause for my reluctance is that I am certain the intelligence community and many others will criticize me for what I reveal. I am curious who will lead this attack and what their motives may be. The impending controversy should help reveal that people are still living who were responsible for the assassination of President John F. Kennedy. For those who avoid the controversy, I question whether they will use the information I reveal to help solve the murder of President Kennedy. Although I include many references to other's first-hand information in this book, a great portion of the information will be from my personal experience.

My son-in-law Jonathan said to me, "you know Hawk, many men have served in the military." He was obviously alluding to my seemingly obsessive preoccupation with the years I spent in the United States Marine Corps. Yes, many men have served, but few have found themselves crouching 2,500 yards from ground zero in a trench on the floor of Mojave Desert being used as a nuclear guinea pig by the US government. Tests that were performed for the sole purpose of testing the effects a nuclear blast would have on military troops in combat. I doubt that any ex-Marine shares my experience of having been on a secret mission in the mountains of Taiwan with Lee Harvey Oswald, the alleged assassin of President John F. Kennedy. Very few former Marines have been used as a mind-controlled type of Manchurian Candidate, but Oswald and I were used when we traveled on a secret mission into the mountains of Taiwan with a group of Chinese military personnel. This mission was at the pinnacle of the Cold War when Communist China was bombing the Kinmen Islands of Quemoy and Matsu. These islands are located between mainland China and just off the coast of Taiwan which is also known as Nationalist

China in the same region of the world where the Vietnam War erupted a few years later.

While serving my country, I carried a sawed-off shotgun while walking guard duty in a typhoon at Atsugi Naval Air Station in Japan protecting the hangar that housed the top-secret U-2 spy plane. This was the same type of plane that pilot Col. Francis Gary Powers was shot down in over Russia just few years later, which was a contributing factor in extending the Cold War. And, I have sent and received messages from President Dwight D. Eisenhower pertaining to the U-2 spy plane while serving in a combat zone. As you can see, I have an abundance of memories and experiences to consider and make known.

Fifty years have passed since I stood as a young recruit on the large asphalt grinder at the Marine Corps Recruit Depot in San Diego, California. It is said one remembers best what is placed in their memory with emphasis and my years in the Marine Corps certainly fall into this category. It has been impossible for me to put the last 50 years to rest as many of the same issues that were significant at that point in time, are still present in our current environment. The Chinese are still in conflict over the control of Taiwan, the CIA is still lying and passing on disinformation, and the assassination of President Kennedy is still an open case. The information contained in this book will provide researchers with the guideposts necessary to assist them in the correct investigative direction. I will not dwell on the specifics of Dealey Plaza or the assassination, nor who committed the act, or how, or why it took place. My intent is to exonerate Lee Harvey Oswald of guilt and complicity in the assassination of President John F. Kennedy, and to illustrate how he was used as a patsy. This book pertains to my life in the US Marine Corps, my relationship with Oswald, and how we were used as mind-controlled subjects by the MKULTRA, the clandestine top-secret division of the CIA.

I enlisted in the Marine Corps in the summer of 1956, just a short time after I turned 18 years old and graduated high school. I completed basic training at the Marine's Recruit Depot in San Diego, California. I later was a member of the Western Division rifle team that represented the Marine Corps from Camp Pendleton, California. In the spring of 1958 I was assigned a new duty station and shipped off to Japan, where I was stationed at the Atsugi Naval Air Station (NAS Atsugi) with the First Marine Air Wing. It was while I was stationed at Atsugi that I met Lee Harvey Oswald.

I was on duty in the communication headquarters at Atsugi, when a flash message was received with orders from President Eisenhower to move MAG 11 from NAS Atsugi in Japan to Pingtung, Formosa, now known as Taiwan The First Marine Air Wing was sent to Taiwan in support of General Chang Kai Shek's military as advances were being made by Mainland China's military. The Republic of China's military was bombing Taiwan's off shore islands of Quemoy and Matsu during the time we were deployed to Pingtung. Fear had been expressed that Mainland China would invade Taiwan, take over the island, and install a communist controlled government.

In the 1950's, NAS Atsugi was known as a spook base as it was headquarters for the CIA's top-secret MKULTRA mind control program as well as its U-2 spy plane project. I was used by the MKULTRA along with other unsuspecting young Marines. I traveled about Japan, Taiwan, Hong Kong, and California under the control of the program as a courier used to deliver top-secret information. This information was either given to me or I may have removed it from Marine message center headquarters in Pingtung and Atsugi without being aware I was stealing it. Many unknowing subjects were also used as infiltrating agents and at least one was used as a patsy. These subjects could also function as hypnotically controlled cameras as it was possible for them to enter a room or building, memorize materials, and then quickly leave. The memorized information could be retrieved by a controller or handler with a previously implanted code or signal. This could all be accomplished without the knowledge or awareness of the subject. In addition to hypnosis, magnetic fields, drugs, sound waves, sleep deprivation, and solitary confinement were also used sometimes by the MKULTRA program doctors.

I returned to the United States after my tour of duty and continued to be controlled by the MKULTRA while in California. During my time there, I spent a weekend or more under the control of the MKULTRA, which took me to Monterey, California. It was here where I may have spent time at the Defense Language Institute. It has been acknowledged by researchers that Oswald had spent time at this same military language school and had participated in a crash course in Russian. Drugs, hypnosis, and subliminal suggestion were used to help accomplish the accelerated pace of the program. In addition to the language school, I believe I was also programmed to be a sleeper. This is an individual programmed to perform tasks by the use of key control words and phrases spoken by a controller to manipulate the individual's actions. I believe I may have been prepared for this use after I returned home from the Far East during my time at the Treasure Island Naval Base in San Francisco. A memorable reference to sleepers appears in the movie *Telefon*. Charles Bronson's character searches for sleepers who had been programmed by the Russian KGB to commit sabotage and clandestine operations at a future date. After hearing the phrase, "stopping by the woods on a snowy evening," the sleepers would carry out specific missions that may take place many years after they had been programmed. It has been rumored that the CIA developed several sleepers.

It is overwhelming at times for me to contemplate all that has transpired in the past 50 years. From the moment I heard the news of the assassination of President Kennedy and realized that I knew the alleged killer, I have worked diligently to try to piece together information and make sense of what really happened on that fateful day in 1963. In

4

the more than 40 years since, I have diligently researched and studied to try and discover the truth surrounding the assassination. Many investigators have tried to solve the mystery from information gathered at the crime scene in Dealey Plaza; however, to understand this crime, it is more important to study the events that led up to the assassination. Knowing the identity of the shooters is not nearly as important as understanding who masterminded the conspiracy. Just as knowing who pulled the trigger is more important than the make or model of rifle used in the crime. I doubt if we will ever know all who may have been involved, but my quest is to work to try and expose as many individuals as I can who may have been responsible. Many benefited from the death of President Kennedy and I question who they were and why they thought it necessary to kill the President. By exonerating Oswald, we will release researchers and investigators to pursue those who are guilty. Numerous conspiracy theories have muddied the investigation waters by entertaining various speculations that it might have been the Hunt family, Vice President Lyndon Johnson, the Mafia, Fidel Castro, the Russians, and the idea that President Kennedy was murdered for stock market manipulation. One familiar theory is that the bullet hit Kennedy by mistake as someone tried to shoot Governor Connelly. There are also numerous theories that involve the picket fence, the grassy knoll, the sixth floor window of the School Book Depository, the bums arrested in the railroad yard, Dallas Police Department, a secret service agent within the presidential limousine, and the billionaire Aristotle Onassis who was to be the future husband of Jacquelyn Kennedy. The amount of disinformation in the public realm about the assassination is astounding and I have no doubt that a group of individuals within the CIA and factions of our own government are responsible for the assassination of President John F. Kennedy. It is for this reason the assassination was never solved, and the real killers have never been brought to justice. With the CIA and the FBI in charge of the investigation, the fox has been guarding the hen house.

This book will lead you systematically through the portion of Oswald's life when he served in the Marine Corps and how he was controlled by the CIA with possible assistance by Naval Intelligence. As you will read, the United States Marine Corps is also complicit in the conspiracy as they would have had to turn a blind eye when Oswald was being used by the MKULTRA. Oswald was also possibly monitored by the FBI when he returned from Russia. After the Kennedy assassination, Oswald made the statement "I am a patsy." However, unbeknownst to him, he was used as a patsy twice. The first incident occurred when he was sent to Russia by the CIA under the control of the MKULTRA. He was accused of passing information to the Russians about the top-secret U-2 spy plane. Hypothetically, this information provided the Russians with the necessary elevation and flight path information to enable them to shoot down the U-2. The second incident was when he was placed in a compromising situation within the Texas School Book Depository. This cover-up was made complete when Jack Ruby killed Oswald. The Dallas Police Department, FBI, President Lyndon Johnson, and the Warren Commission then covered up the rest of the mess. Mission accomplished!

I am amazed at how many Marines who were stationed at NAS Atsugi, were also linked in various ways to the Kennedy assassination. This book will help illustrate the connection between the Marine Corps, NAS Atsugi, the CIA and its MKULTRA program, Naval Intelligence, and the responsibility of each group in the conspiracy. While performing my research, I discovered Jerry Leonard's book, *The Perfect Assassin.* Leonard writes a compelling story about the MKULTRA and its control of unknowing and unwilling subjects. Although this book presents a wonderful hypothesis of a controlled assassin, it represents the true story of my life, and that of Oswald's, as controlled Marines.

Oswald was, as he declared, a patsy.

Preface

My son-in-law Eric remarked, "Hawk you know you are never going to solve the Kennedy assassination." Of course I agree with him, but in this book I present a good deal of new and significant information that should send researchers off on a renewed pursuit for the truth. This information may be some of the most pertinent information yet to be released with regards to Oswald and his connection to the intelligence community. These facts have never before been presented and are a first person account of what happened to Oswald and me in 1958 and 1959.

On November 22, 1963, a very powerful and well-financed group of individuals culminated a conspiracy that killed President John F. Kennedy, and then engaged in a massive cover-up that prevented the public from learning the truth. This same group of individuals have surfaced in other very serious transgressions. The Phoenix Program, Watergate break-in, Bay of Pigs Invasion, Iran Contra affair, and the Bank of Commerce and Credit International scandal, are just a few of these crimes. The individuals who assassinated President Kennedy must still have enough power in the government and media to enable them to keep a cover-up in place. Many of these individuals are now deceased, but those that are not, have inherited the cover-up of these crimes in order to keep the truth hidden. After the passage of the Freedom of Information Act, many, but not all, documents pertaining to this cover-up were released. Several of these documents had pages blacked-out or deleted as they were still considered a risk to national security. It is difficult to believe that anything that happened in 1963 would continue to negatively impact our current national security. I contend that individuals that still hold positions within our government continue to be protected by the cover-up. It is a shame that a few powerful people persist in holding onto their positions and legacy, while innocent people have gone to their graves as apparent villains.

Many excellent books have been written about the assassination of President John F. Kennedy. However, in my research I have found only a few books that have mentioned the Atsugi Naval Air Station in Japan (NAS Atsugi). This military base, and the CIA's MKULTRA mind-control program were in full operation while I was stationed there. I am certain that NAS Atsugi and the MKULTRA are two of the most important pieces in the assassination puzzle. Through my personal experiences, I will implicate the CIA and Naval Intelligence as well as the United States Marine Corps (USMC) as being complicit in the assassination by their control of Oswald through brainwashing. The USMC knew what was happening to me and Oswald, and many others, and allowed the MKULTRA to use us for their mind-control experiments. Oswald was brainwashed and controlled while he was stationed at NAS Atsugi. At this same time, the MKULTRA operated at Atsugi and tried to construct a Manchurian Candidate. They succeeded with Lee Harvey Oswald.

Far too many people involved in the Kennedy assassination have ties to NAS Atsugi for it to be mere coincidence. Understanding what happened at this mysterious base in the mid to late 1950s will give one a better perspective as to what Oswald meant when he uttered the infamous "I am a patsy" statement after his arrest. Only a few days after he had allegedly assassinated President Kennedy, Oswald was expediently eliminated by Jack Ruby. Unfortunately, he was murdered before he could explain his "I am a patsy" statement.

In the 1950s, NAS Atsugi housed the top-secret U-2 spy plane. This was the same type of aircraft that was involved in an international incident when it was shot down over the Soviet Union in 1960. The U-2 was piloted by Colonel Fracis Gary Powers and was brought down while on a supposed spy mission. This incident took place just prior to the Paris Summit between President Eisenhower and Nikita Krushchev. Shortly before this event, Eisenhower had denied the US was flying reconnaissance missions over Russia. The incident left Eisenhower in an embarrassing situation and was instrumental in extending the Cold War. The US Government later blamed Oswald for his part in this affair and accused him of passing pertinent information to the Russians that enabled them to analyze the altitude and flight patterns of the U-2.

At this same time, NAS Atsugi was also the Far East headquarters for the CIA. It was regarded as a Spook Base because of the top-secret programs operating there that included the MKULTRA mind-control program. This program was designed to use innocent and unsuspecting young Marines for various types of missions. This was done through a combination of drugs and many times hypnosis was also used. If a programmed Marine were discovered or captured, they would have no knowledge of their mission and could present a total and honest denial.

The term "Manchurian Candidate" was coined by author Richard Condon in his book by the same name. It's premise centered on a serviceman who had been brainwashed into becoming an unwilling assassin. I do not believe that Oswald was the first "Manchurian Candidate", just the best known. The US Government should clear Oswald of Kennedy's assassination and reinstate his Honorable Discharge given to him by the United States Marine Corps. Several decades have passed since this terrible crime and it is time to correct a wrong, however difficult it may be, and find the President's true assassins.

The men who served on the Warren Commission are always referred to as honorable men. How honorable is it to overlook and change pertinent information and damaging testimony in order to arrive at a foregone conclusion? This foregone conclusion was that Oswald was a dysfunctional "lone-nut" who had assassinated President Kennedy because of some deep and complex emotional need to be recognized. The Warren Commission merely needed to use disinformation and twist evidence to make the pieces fit. An excellent example of misinterpreted evidence is illustrated by Arlen Spector's ridiculous single magic bullet theory. This misinformation, coupled with Gerald Ford's alteration of records to change the bullet entry wound by three inches to coincide with Specter's theory, has helped keep the American public from the truth.

Former Senator Richard Schweiker had declared, "I personally believe that he (Oswald) had a special relationship with one of the intelligence agencies, which one I'm not certain. But all the fingerprints I found during my 18 months on the Senate Select Committee on Intelligence point to Oswald as being a product of, and interacting with, the intelligence community."

After months of investigation, the honorable men of the Warren Commission determined that Oswald was the lone assassin of President Kennedy. The information you are about read will challenge that conclusion.

Chapter One

Atsugi Naval Air Station

THIS IS

The Ship I Sailed On

USS General A. E. Anderson

One does not want to board a ship in January and have their destination be the Far East. The Pacific Ocean in January is not a friendly place. I was a nineteen year old Marine in the spring of 1958 when I boarded the USS General A. E. Anderson, a troop ship, and embarked from a port in Los Angles, California, on what was called the January draft. We were all designated to replace the Marines who were returning home after having served their allotted time. As 'replacement' Marines, were assigned specific jobs. I was trained as a teletype operator and was transferred to fill a position at the headquarters of Atsugi Naval Air Station in Japan. We boarded the USS Anderson after having spent approximately one month at the El Toro Marine Air Base (MCAS El Toro) near Santa Anna, California. At El Toro we received inoculations and processing information that would prepare us for our future tour of duty in the Far East.

We arrived at port in Yokohama, Japan, and waiting dock-side was a Navy bus designated to be our ride to Atsugi Naval Air Station that would be our new home for the next two years. We arrived at Atsugi shortly before dusk; therefore, I have a limited first impression of the base.

NAS Atsugi is located twenty miles from Tokyo situated on Honshu, the main island of Japan and is positioned in the heart of the Kanto Plain, on approximately 1,250 acres. The nearest liberty or off duty destination for most Marines was a small village named Yomotomachi, which is a couple of miles from Atsugi's rear gate. Atsugi is elevated above the surrounding area on a plateau and the land below the base consisted of farms covered with rice paddies. The station was built in 1938 by the Japanese Imperial Navy at the request of Emperor Hirohito to thwart the possibility of future bombing raids by American planes on the Japanese mainland. The site was originally used as a training base for the Emperor's pilots from the 302 Naval Aviation Corps, who flew the Zero and Gekko fighter planes. These planes were considered the most formidable factor in the Japanese air defense system during World War II. The First and Second Sagamino Naval Air Group used the Atsugi airfield for strategic night missions and were also responsible for building underground facilities under the base. It is rumored that during the late 1950's, and while under American supervision, the underground facilities and numerous nearby caves housed nuclear weapons in clear violation of Japanese law. The training facility at Atsugi under the command of Captain Yasuna Kozono was recognized as the top aviation base in Japan; only the most elite pilots flew from Atsugi.

On August 15, 1945, with the acceptance of the Potsdam Declaration, Emperor Hirohito announced that Japan would unconditionally surrender. Many groups throughout Japan refused to accept the surrender and among them were Captain Yasuna Kozono and his pilots at Atsugi. Captain Kozono and his pilots vowed to defend mainland Japan to the very end. The pilots revolted and dropped thousands of leaflets over Tokyo, Yokohama, Yokosuka, and other locations around the Kanto Plain. The leaflets stated that those that surrendered were guilty of treason, thereby urging the continuation of the war. This group held Atsugi captive for seven days, but flew out on 33 planes when they realized that surrender was a reality.

On August 30, 1945, General Douglas MacArthur landed at Atsugi to accept the formal Japanese surrender which took place aboard the USS Missouri. At this time General MacArthur also assumed duties as Military Governor of Japan. It was prior to MacArthur's arrival that 4,200 troops from Okinawa carried by 123 planes landed at the airstrip at Atsugi. The war had ended, and all the prisoners from the caves and holding facilities around the base were released. During the following five years, Atsugi was used by the United States Army as a storage area.

On June 25, 1950, at the outbreak of the Korean War, Atsugi was selected by the Navy as its major Naval Air Station in the Far East and on December 1, 1950, Naval Air Station Atsugi was commissioned. On March 7, 1953, a lone plane landed at Atsugi with a large group of United Nations wounded troops that were on route to the Naval Hospital at Yokosuka. This was the first time Atsugi had been the receiving point for Korean War evacuees and conflicts in the Far East developed into the Vietnam War, the Naval Air Station (NAS) at Atsugi again became a very integral base in the Far East. In 1958, Atsugi was home to the First Marine Air Wing, and the home of the top-secret U-2 spy plane.

In April of 1969, Atsugi was involved in an international confrontation which placed the entire world on alert. A reconnaissance plane assigned to squadron VQ-1 at Atsugi was shot down over the Sea of Japan. The plane was shot down by two North Korean MiG-17 fighters and all 31 Navy personnel aboard perished. Atsugi NAS became an extremely busy military base when President Richard Nixon, because of the incident, ordered an armada of Navy ships to assemble in the Sea of Japan. The personnel at Atsugi worked diligently to give logistical support to the 29 ships. Gradually the tense situation eased and the ships returned to normal duties. In 1972, the USS Midway was deployed to

Yokosuka, and Atsugi became a support base for its Air Wing. The area around Atsugi in the following years has experienced a population explosion which brought considerable encroachment that presently exists around the base.

The Sagamino train station is approximately one mile from Atsugi's main gate, providing a thirty minute ride to Yokohama, and an hour ride to Tokyo. The rear gate and entry to the Carrier Air Wing Five is approximately one mile from the Japanese city of Yamato. I clearly recall walking a guard duty post around the top-secret U-2 plane the night the old train station in Yamatomachi burned to the ground.

The correct title for Atsugi is currently Naval Air Facility Atsugi; it is the largest Naval Air Facility in the Far East, and current and only home to Carrier Air Wing 5. Carrier Air Wing Five has 10 squadrons, which operate eight different types of aircraft that share a single runway. The runway and hangers are situated between the Marine and Navy side of Atsugi.

Atsugi was not a large base; it was divided into two sections, one being the Navy or main side which was connected by a single road to the much smaller Marine side. The barrack area on the Marine Corps side encompassed an area equivalent to four city blocks. It contained billets (sleeping quarters), and a combination football, baseball, and exercise field. There were additional buildings, including a nondenominational church, an enlisted men's club, mess hall, library, a special service and supply building, and a Marine Wing headquarters where I would work. This area was populated by only a few hundred Marines. When I arrived at Atsugi most of the First Marine Air Wing, including Lee Harvey Oswald, were on maneuvers in the Philippines; therefore, only a skeleton crew remained.

My Military Occupation Specialty, or MOS 2511, placed me in the Marine Headquarters office as a teletype operator. I had just graduated from teletype school at Marine Corps Recruit Depot in San Diego, California, and my rank was a Private First Class. My first duty station had been the 5th Marines at Camp Pendleton, California, after which I was transferred to the base headquarters on Camp Pendleton.

I was working at the Camp Pendleton headquarters when we received a message from Japan requesting someone with my MOS to fill an upcoming MOS 2511 vacancy in Japan. I immediately removed the message from the teletype machine and hand-delivered it to the commanding General and requested the opportunity to fill the position. My request was approved and a few days later I departed for Wisconsin on a 30-day home leave prior to my new duty assignment in Japan.

While working in the message center headquarters at Atsugi, I attended another teletype school at Marine Corps Air Station Iwakuni, Japan, on the main Island of Honshu. This school prepared me to be a message center supervisor upon my return to Atsugi. While at Iwakuni I had the opportunity to visit Hiroshima, the site of the Atomic Bomb explosion that brought an end to World War II. Interestingly, in 1957 I was stationed with the Fifth Marines at Camp Pendleton, California, and was used as a nuclear guinea pig; witnessing a nuclear detonation while kneeling in a trench 2500 yards from ground zero. This blast was five times larger than the bomb dropped on Hiroshima, and the largest ever detonated in the continental United States. My visit to Hiroshima ground zero brought me full circle from the Nevada test site. The area in Nevada where we were witness to the atomic bomb detonation is now part of the top-secret infamous Area 51. I mention this as the human nuclear experimentation program was yet another of the MKULTRA programs. Once again I had been exposed to the MKULTRA and its mind control program that was currently in full development at Atsugi. This exposure causes me to question if my time spent as a member on the Western Division rifle team was also a segment of my MKULTRA training.

Upon my return from teletype school in Iwakuni, I was notified that each squadron was required to provide one Marine to serve on mess duty. As I held the lowest rank in the Headquarters Message Center, and had spent the least amount of time in the Far East, I was selected for the 30-day assignment. While on mess duty I met another young Marine who was stationed with the Marine Air Squadron One (MACS1). This young Marine's name was Lee Harvey Oswald, the now alleged assassin of President John F. Kennedy.

Oswald worked in the Atsugi air control tower charting the departures, arrivals, elevations, and missions of the top-secret U-2 spy plane. The control tower personnel at the Atsugi air strip would monitor flights of the U-2 spy plane over China and Russia. So top-secret were these flights, they would only depart on direct orders from President Eisenhower. I recall the first time I inquired as to what was housed in these heavily guarded hangars; I was told the hangars housed B-one-RD'S. It was their humorous way of saying "birds" and letting me know it was none of my concern.

Unknown to Oswald and me, at this same point in time Atsugi was the CIA's Far East headquarters and sheltered its top-secret MKULTRA mind control program that was started on the order of CIA Director Allen Dulles. The MKULTRA was a research program that experimented with mind control using a combination of hypnosis and drugs which were used either alone or in combination. The MKULTRA mind control subjects included young men from the United States Marine Corps who were most often unwitting victims in these experiments.

Knowledge of this mind control program is especially disturbing when you consider that one of the young Marines stationed at Atsugi, who was victimized by the CIA and their mind control program, later became the accused assassin of President John F. Kennedy. The CIA and the Warren Commission selectively chose Oswald as the person responsible for assassinating the President; they needed a "patsy."

By revealing information regarding the MKULTRA and what was taking place at Atsugi Naval Air Station, I will expose one of the greatest cover-ups the CIA, FBI, ONI, United States Marine Corps, and the Warren Commission supporters have concealed these many years. There are also other organizations and numerous individuals who were involved and responsible for the strategy, implementation, and cover up of the assassination of John F. Kennedy who have kept the mind control program a secret. One must remember that this was a government intelligence agency of the highest order that used drugs and hypnosis to control an unsuspecting young Atsugi Marine's life. Oswald had become a real life Manchurian Candidate while he was stationed at the Atsugi Naval Air Station in Japan.

Chapter Two

Central Intelligence Agency (CIA)

The intelligence community has never been more closely scrutinized than since the 9/11 attacks against the United States that included the total destruction of the World Trade Center in New York City. An internal review of the CIA's performance surrounding these attacks was carried out to investigate personnel both before and after the attacks. This investigation resulted in the creation of the 9/11 Commission whose report found that both the CIA and FBI failed to identify important intelligence information that may have prevented the attacks. Because of faulty intelligence, and the Bush Administration's creation of a link between the 9/11 attacks and Saddam Hussein, the U.S. was led into the Iraq war. There was to have been a complete revamp of the intelligence community brought about by these debacles, yet it seems as though the same good old boys are still running the show and it is apparent that even after all these years, it is still business as usual.

The Central Intelligence Agency is best known by the initials CIA, and as "The Company," by its employees. Agents within the CIA are known as "spooks" and hired assassins are known as "Mechanics." The origin of the CIA came about under President Franklin D. Roosevelt in 1941 when the war with Japan and Germany forced the United States to form an intelligence gathering organization. Previous to 1941, during Abraham Lincoln's presidency, Allan Pinkerton was hired to manage the Northern spy organization for the government. Interestingly, after the Civil War Pinkerton went on to form the Pinkerton Detective Agency. Between the Lincoln presidency and the next presidential term there were basically no intelligence gathering organizations. In 1942, President Roosevelt appointed William "Wild Bill" Donavan to head the Office of Strategic Services (OSS), the predecessor of the CIA. Donavan, a Columbia University

Alumni, was a decorated First World War hero, a millionaire Wall Street lawyer, and an active member of the Republican Party. Donavan recruited his intelligence agents from socially connected and privileged young men from Ivy League colleges. Similarly, the British counterparts to the CIA, the M15 and M16, recruited their intelligence agents from Oxford and Cambridge. Because of the CIA's recruitment from Ivy League colleges, the rumor persists that the CIA is part and parcel of highly secret organizations within these colleges such as the Skull and Bones Club at Yale University, and the Scroll and Key at Harvard University.

President Truman ordered the OSS to be closed after the Second World War leaving only a small investigative entity, the Strategic Service Unit (SSU), intact. Despite being closed, the OSS was a template for the CIA that was established in 1947. At this time, the newly formed agency was forbidden from operating within the U.S. upon the request of J. Edgar Hoover, director of the Federal Bureau of Investigation (FBI). It is believed that Hoover was concerned that he and the FBI would lose the power of investigation to the CIA.

In the final stages of the Second World War, the OSS engaged in a mad scramble with the Russians to acquire intelligence information and recruit agents from groups of German scientists. This recruitment fell under the code name "Operation Paperclip." The War Department's Joint Intelligence Objectives Agency (JOIA) conducted background investigations and formed dossiers on the scientists. The JOIA found that a majority of these scientists had been deeply involved in the Nazi party and had been involved in horrific war crimes that included human experiments.

President Truman ordered that no committed Nazis be admitted under Operation Paperclip. However, CIA director Alan Dulles met with Nazi Intelligence leader Reinhart Gehlen and promised that his Intelligence network was safe in the CIA and had the scientist's dossiers rewritten to remove incriminating evidence. Unfortunately, President Truman was never aware that his command had been violated. The clandestine pact between Dulles and Gehlen allowed Nazi intelligence to be delivered to the CIA and was the catalyst for many experimental mind control projects that stemmed from Nazi research such as Project Bluebird, Project Artichoke, Operation Midnight Climax, and the MK-ULTRA.

Another clandestine organization, the ODESSA network, was also created to aid fugitive Nazis and helped them move to Canada, South America, Central America, and the US under the blind eye of the CIA. According to Simon Wiesenthal, ODESSA was created in 1946 and helped Dr. Josef Mengele, known as the Angel of Death, and Adolf Eichmann, who sent more than four hundred thousand Jews to their deaths in gas chambers, escape to South America. Wiesenthal dedicated most of his life to tracking down fugitive Nazis so that they could be brought to justice.

Over the past few years during the process of writing this book, I have discovered that new information is continuously being revealed even at this late date, primarily because of the passing of the U. S. Freedom of Information Act (FOIA). The FOIA was signed into law by President Lyndon B. Johnson on July 4, 1966 (*Amended 2002*), and went into effect the following year and allows public access to previously unreleased U.S. Government information and documents. For example, a document illustrates that in 1960, at the request of West Germany, the CIA persuaded Life Magazine, which had purchased Adolf Eichmann's memoir, to delete a reference to Hans Globke before publication. Globke helped created the legislation that gave Hilter unlimited dictatorial powers and revoked the citizenship of German Jews.

The following article appeared in the St. Paul Pioneer Press on June 7, 2006, long after I had completed this chapter. It is written by Scott Shane of the New York Times and titled "CIA knew of Holocaust Planners Whereabouts."

The CIA took no action after learning the pseudonym and whereabouts of the fugitive Holocaust administrator Adolf Eichmann in 1958, according to CIA documents released Tuesday that shed new light on the spy agency's use of former Nazis as informants after World War II.

The CIA was told by West German intelligence that Eichmann was living in Argentina under the name Clemens in a slight variation of his actual alias, Ricardo Klement—but did not share the information with Israel which had been hunting for him for years, according to Timothy Naftali, a historian who examined the documents. These are the honorable men we are to believe, and trust.

Two years later, Israeli agents abducted Eichmann in Argentina and flew him to Israel, where he was tried and executed in 1962.

The Eichmann papers are among 27,000 newly declassified pages released by the CIA to the National Archives under congressional pressure to make public files about former officials of Hitler's regime later used as American agents.

The material reinforces the view that most former Nazi's gave American intelligence little of value and in some cases proved to be damaging double agents for the soviet KGB, according to historians and members of the government panel that has worked to open the long secret files.

Elizabeth Holtzman, a former congress woman from New York and member of the panel, said the documents showed the CIA "failed to lift a finger" to hunt Eichmann.

The U.S. government, preoccupied with the Cold War, had no policy at the time of pursuing Nazi war criminals. The records also show that American Intelligence officials protected many former Nazi's for their perceived value in combating the Soviet threat.

But Holtzman, speaking at a press briefing at the National Archives on Tuesday, said information from the former Nazis often tainted both by their "personal agendas" and their vulnerability to blackmail. "Using bad people can have very bad consequences," Holtzman said. She and other group members suggested that the findings should be a cautionary guide for intelligence agencies today.

Documents illustrate that in 1960, also at the request of West Germany, the CIA persuaded Life Magazine, which had purchased Eichmann's memoir from his family, to delete a reference to Globke before publication. It was also Life Magazine that purchased the Abraham Zapruder film showing the assassination in Dealey Plaza of President John F. Kennedy. Three copies were made the same day of the assassinations. Life magazine purchased the original for $150, 000 to be paid to Zapruder in six annual payments of $25,000. The value Life magazine paid in today's dollar would be almost $1,000,000. Frames have been shown individually by Life magazine. The film has been locked away from public scrutiny and was never publicly shown in motion by Life magazine.

Ironically, in view of the information the CIA received in 1958, documents previously released by the CIA showed that it was taken by surprise in May 1960 when the Israelis captured Eichmann. Cables from the time show that (Allen Dulles), the

CIA director, demanded that officers find out more about the capture of his friends.

Norman J. W. Goda, an Ohio University historian reviewed the CIA material, and said it shows in greater detail than was previously known that the KGB aggressively recruited former Nazi intelligence officers after the war.

The documents also provide new information about the case of Tscherim Soobzokov, a former Nazi SS officer who was the subject of a much publicized deportation case in 1979 when he was living as an American citizen in Patterson, N.J. He was charged with having falsified his immigration application to conceal his SS service, which ordinarily would have barred his entry, but the charge was dropped when a CIA document turned up showing that he had disclosed his SS membership; how convenient.

The newly declassified records show that Soobzokov was employed by the CIA from 1952 to 1959 despite "clear evidence of a war crimes record" said another historian at the briefing, Richard Breitman of American University.

Because it valued Soobzokov for his language skills and ties to fellow ethnic Circassians living in the Soviet Union the CIA deliberately hid details of his Nazi record from the Immigration and Naturalization Service after he moved to the United States in 1955, Breitman said. But Soobzokov ultimately did not escape his past. He died in 1985 after a pipe bomb exploded outside his house. The case has never been solved.

Note that in this article, Allen Dulles, director of CIA and father of the MKULTRA mind-control program, seems to be lying and covering up information dating back to

World War II. The article also notes how the CIA came up with a loophole for Nazi Soobzokov to stay in the US by saying he had disclosed he had been a member of the Nazi party. It was also previously noted that Life Magazine purchased the Eichmann memoirs; they were also the magazine that bought the Abraham Zapruder film of the Kennedy assassination. What is going on behind the closed doors of Life Magazine?

In 1953 Allen Dulles became director of the CIA at the same time his brother John Foster Dulles was serving as Secretary of State in President Dwight Eisenhower's administration. Allen Dulles was later fired by President John F. Kennedy over the Bay of Pigs fiasco that had been set in motion during the Eisenhower administration. This program was overseen by Vice President Richard Nixon and managed by Dulles who was later appointed by President Lyndon B. Johnson to serve on the Warren Commission to investigate President Kennedy's assassination. President Johnson's decision was probably dictated by the real leader of the United States, the intelligence community.

President John F. Kennedy made a fatal mistake when he said he was going to splinter the CIA into a million parts and scatter them to the wind; this comment may have cost him his life. President Kennedy made another fatal mistake in thinking that the President is in control of the government and not understanding the power and danger in confronting the intelligence community.

According to William Corson in his book *Armies of Ignorance*, President James E. Carter had made the same statement regarding the breakup of the CIA. Corson notes that President Carter had been so naïve that when he assumed the presidency, he did not know that King Hussein of Jordan was a CIA Operative. I, too, was also not aware of King Hussein's CIA connection when I was serving in a combat zone in Pingtung, Taiwan. This information by William Corson helped me to understand a question that had been nagging me for almost 50 years. What was King Hussein doing in Taiwan in 1958 during the time Communist China was bombing the Kinmen, Quemoy, and Matsu islands? It had to be his CIA connection that brought him to Taiwan during this crisis and into such a potential precarious situation.

In the early 1990's, when the United States was engaged in the first golf war with Iraq, President George H. W. Bush requested permission to use flight space over the country of Jordan. King Hussein denied this request. It is interesting that King Hussein, a CIA operative, denied this request from former President Bush who had been a CIA director. Over the years, an explanation has fallen together. King Hussein was married to an American woman and owned a home which was located on the shore of the Potomac River in the state of Maryland. Air America was the largest private airline in the world, and was operated by the CIA, based in Taipei, Taiwan. Additionally, the U-2 spy plane and MKULTRA programs were based in Atsugi, Japan. The CIA was operating full force in the Far East, and King Hussein viewed this as our intelligence unit in action.

It is said by many that the Vietnam War began the very day the Korean War ended. In 1968, the CIA began operating full force in Cambodia under the Phoenix Program. This program was designed to bring together the police, military and other government organizations to disrupt the civilian infrastructure by capturing or killing the Viet Cong. The Phoenix Program was often called an "assassination campaign," and is an example of human rights atrocities alleged to have been committed by the CIA or other allied organizations.

The deceit and interference into other country's governments runs deep within the intelligence community, and was still evident in the misinformation surrounding the Weapons of Mass Destruction (WMD) that supposedly existed in Iraq. This party line led to the invasion of Iraq, the loss of thousands of American and Iraq lives, and billions of dollars spent with an end still not in sight. This massive boondoggle has been spun into a quest for democracy for the Iraq people, but no one is being held accountable. CIA Director George Tenet, responsible for the erroneous information on WMD, retired with full government pension and was awarded the Freedom Medal by President George W. Bush. Through disinformation, misinformation, and fear, the American people are being misled down a very dangerous path.

President John F. Kennedy lost his life because he felt that the CIA should be dismantled. He fired CIA Director Allen Dulles over the Bay of Pigs fiasco, and also intended to deescalate the Vietnam conflict which would affect the lucrative military establishment. It was also rumored that Kennedy was not going to include Vice President Lyndon Johnson on his reelection ticket, and was sympathetic with the plight of the African American people. It is now forty-four years after Kennedy's assassination, the talk is on-going as to how to restructure the CIA. I believe the same people will remain in control, and things will only appear to change as The Company is too big and powerful and is underwritten by our very own tax dollars. The American people need to take back their country from these self appointed so called intelligent people.

Chapter Three

MKULTRA

In the fall of 2004 I was in Pia, Thailand, enjoying a massage in a small bamboo hut. The individual lying on a massage mat nearby was a retired psychology professor from a major United States university. He mentioned that he had spent the past 40 years teaching students how to be guidance counselors at the high school level. As our conversation drifted, and because of his psychology background, I asked him what he knew about the MKULTRA program. He was puzzled by the question and stated that he had never heard of the MKULTRA, and questioned me as to what I was referring. I was surprised that this gentleman, who had spent the majority of his life studying and working within a prominent university's psychology department, remained unaware of the government's mind control program. I was especially puzzled because it was revealed through congressional hearings that more than thirty universities and institutions were involved in the program which included secret drug tests on unwitting human subjects at all social and economic levels.

The MKULTRA was the mind control section of the Central Intelligence Agency (CIA). One should probably not use the past tense as the MKULTRA is most likely alive and well and operating under another title such as the Star Gate program. The MKULTRA was conceived by Richard Helms of the Clandestine Services Department. It is said that "MK" may possibly stand for "Mind Kontrolle," and the German translation of Kontrolle into English is "control."

Dr. Joseph Mengele of Auschwitz notoriety and a member of the Nazi party in Germany should also get credit for being the primary developer of the MKULTRA and the Monarch mind control programs. In fact, many of the members of the MKULTRA were once part of Germany's

Nazis party. Mengele, the Angel of Death, and hundreds of other high ranking Nazis were secretly shuttled into the US and South America after World War II. The code name for protecting and moving Nazi war criminals out of Germany was titled Operation Paperclip.

On April 13, 1953, Allen Dulles approved the ultra sensitive project titled MKULTRA. Interestingly, President Kennedy fired him from his position as director of the CIA in 1961. The Dulles firing, the Bay of Pigs invasion of Cuba, the statement about dismantling the CIA, along with de-escalation of the Vietnam War is probably what signed President Kennedy's death warrant.

Even though Allen Dulles was fired by Kennedy just prior to the President's assassination, Dulles was still appointed by President Lyndon B. Johnson to serve on the Warren Commission following the assassination. Allen Dulles was the director of the Central Intelligence Agency during the time the MKULTRA was operating at Atsugi Naval Air Station in Japan. As previously mentioned, Atsugi served as CIA headquarters in the Far East. It was at Atsugi that unsuspecting military personnel were used in the mind control experiments associated with the newly formed MKULTRA program. There is an overt connection between the people who were at Atsugi Naval Air Station during the time of Oswald's service and who were also present at Dealey Plaza on November 22, 1963. There are far too many coincidences to be cast off as mere chance.

One must acknowledge the roles that Atsugi, Allen Dulles, the MKULTRA, James Angleton, Richard Bissel, David Atlee Phillips, and Richard Helms played in order to solve the Kennedy assassination. It must be noted that the word MKULTRA and reference to the U-2 spy plane cannot be found in the Warren Commission report. With Oswald so deeply involved with both programs, it is most unusual that it was not investigated. This is a strange omission when one considers that the Warren Commission delved deeply into his childhood that had absolutely nothing to do with anything pertinent to the assassination. Perhaps they were trying to construct a particular conclusion for the assassination? Honorable men would never try to prove an innocent man guilty, but of course Oswald was already dead and presumed guilty, so what did it really matter.

NAS Atsugi was known as a Spook Base during the time Oswald was stationed there. It was also home to another MKULTRA project, the top-secret U-2 spy plane program. The fact that Oswald was stationed at Atsugi at the same time the MKULTRA mind control program was operating there should indicate that it was much more than coincidence. There has been inference made from some researchers that there may, indeed, have been a connection between the MKULTRA program and Oswald. I maintain that Oswald was programmed by the MKULTRA to be in certain places and perform specialized duties without any knowledge or memory of what he had been programmed to carry out.

I am familiar with this program as I was stationed with Oswald at Atsugi, and was ill-treated, drugged, and manipulated by the MKULTRA. I have spent a great deal of the past 50 years trying to piece together how the MKULTRA had used and taken advantage of me. I was sent on missions to apparently deliver and retrieve information for the CIA, in Japan, Hong Kong, California, and in the mountains of Taiwan.

In 1953, Allen Dulles made a public statement on the subject of Communist brain-washing. He stated, "We in the West are somewhat handicapped in getting all the details." He declared, "There are few survivors, and we have no human guinea pigs to try these extra ordinary techniques." At this same time Dulles had given orders to the CIA to find scientists and human guinea pigs in order to begin mind control experiments. The MKULTRA then began using both informed and uninformed military personnel with an ultimate goal of constructing a type of Manchurian Candidate. It has been stated the MKULTRA had developed approximately 20 so-called Manchurian Candidates during this time made up of men who could be controlled, placed in certain compromising situations, and have little or no knowledge of what they had done or what had taken place. This was accomplished through the use of hypnosis, drugs, or a combination of both. Former CIA Director Richard Helms stated in his Senate testimony, "the clandestine operator is trained to believe you can't count on the honesty of your agent to do exactly what you want, or to report accurately unless you own him body, and soul." I have been concerned for many years that the CIA may have turned me into a sleeper, to be used at a later date. Robert and I are living proof that the MKULTRA program existed contrary to Allen Dulles' assertion that it did not. Therefore, the Honorable Allen Dulles did lie.

To quote the classic phrase, "everyone thinks I am paranoid," I do not have total recall of exactly what the MKULTRA may have programmed me to perform. Therefore, I take no chances. I leave when a political candidate or high ranking government official visits the area where I live. I do not want to experience the same terrible fate that befell Oswald and do not want to be placed in a compromising position to later be accused by the powers in control and found guilty of a crime I did not commit.

If one has seen the movie *Conspiracy Theory* staring actors Mel Gibson and Julia Roberts, you will understand how I feel. Mel Gibson's character was tracked by the intelligence community by triggering an alarm in headquarters every time he purchased the book "Catcher in The Rye." This is the same book that Mark David Chapman was obsessed with before he killed John Lennon. The intelligence men in the movie raided Gibson's apartment and found a wall plastered with information regarding the government and its secret antics. Gibson's character recalls later in the movie how he was used by the MKULTRA mind control program to kill a Federal Judge that was Julia Robert's character's father. I site this example because if my home were raided they would find a similar situation. My home is one large John F. Kennedy assassination, CIA, and MKULTRA library. I have newspaper articles, books, pictures, software, and letters; some of which date back prior to Kennedy's assassination. If I were to be investigated, friends and relatives would probably say that I was preoccupied, to the point of obsession, over the Kennedy assassination and Oswald. However, I am not preoccupied; all of my books and papers have served as valuable research tools.

In his book *Spiritism*, Dr. G. H. Estabrooks, a Rhodes Scholar and a psychologist at Colgate College in upstate New York, worked in the MKULTRA program and publicly acknowledged the building of a Manchurian Candidate. Dr. Estabrooks acknowledged that hypnosis did not work on everyone and that only one person in five made a good enough subject to be placed in a deep trance, or state of somnambulism Dr. Estabrooks is described as a former consultant for the FBI and CIA. In a May 13, 1968, article in the *Providence Evening Bulletin*, he was quoted as saying that, "the key to creating an effective spy or assassin rests on splitting a man's personality, or creating a multi-personality, with the aid of hypnotism. This is not science fiction; this has, and is being done. I have done it" said Estabrooks.

Dr. Estabrooks proposed to the CIA on June 22, 1954, that,

> "In deep hypnosis the subject, military or civilian, can be given a message to be delivered to say, Colonel X in Berlin. The message will be perfectly safe and delivered to the proper person because the subject will have no memory whatsoever in the waking state as to the message. It can be arranged that the subject will have no knowledge of ever having been hypnotized. It can be arranged that no one beside Colonel X in Berlin can hypnotize the subject and recover the message. I will take a number

of men and will establish in them through the use of hypnotism the condition of split personality. Consciously they will be dedicated Communists, fanatical advocates to the party line. (Doesn't this sound like the programmed Oswald?) Unconsciously they will be loyal Americans determined to thwart the Communists at every turn. These men will have no knowledge of ever having been hypnotized, and can only be hypnotized by such persons as the original operator may choose. Consciously they will associate with the Communists and learn all their plans. Once every month they, as loyal Americans, will tell what they know. This sounds unbelievable, but I assure you, it will work."

Dr. Estabrooks, in a 1971 article in *Science Digest*, claimed to have created hypnotic couriers and counterintelligence agents for operational use. I know that I was a hypnotic courier while I was stationed at Atsugi, Japan, and in Taiwan. I am certain Oswald was also a hypnotic courier, when I joined him on a secret Chinese Military mission in the mountains of Taiwan in 1958. Oswald could not have been in control of himself as he was a very young low-ranked Marine without the capacity to be in charge of what he was involved. Estabrooks stated,

> "The hypnotic courier provides a unique solution. I was involved in preparing army subjects for this work during World War II. One successful case involved an Army Captain. He was an excellent subject but did not realize it. I removed from him, by post hypnotic suggestion, all recollection of ever having been hypnotized. I put him under deep hypnosis, and gave him orally a vital message to be delivered directly on his arrival in Japan to a certain colonel, let's say his name was Brown-of military intelligence. Outside of myself, Colonel Brown was the only person who could hypnotize Captain Smith. This is called locking. I performed it by say-

ing to the captain, 'We will use the phrase 'the moon is clear. Whenever you hear this phrase from Brown or myself you will pass instantly into deep hypnosis.' When Captain Smith re-awakened, he had no conscious memory of what happened in trance. The system is virtually foolproof."

Estabrooks said that by the 1920's, clinical hypnotists had learned to apply posthypnotic suggestions and had also learned to split certain complex individuals into multiple personalities much like the fictional Jeckyl and Hyde. He states,

> "During World War II, I worked this technique with a vulnerable Marine lieutenant I'll call Jones. I split his personality into Jones A and Jones B, Jones A, once a "normal" working Marine, became entirely different. He talked communist doctrine and meant it. He was welcomed enthusiastically by communist cells, and was deliberately given dishonorable discharge by the Corps and became a card-carrying party member. Jones B was the deeper personality, knew all the thoughts of Jones A, was a loyal American and was "imprinted" to say nothing during conscious phases. All I had to do was hypnotize the whole man, get in touch with Jones B, the loyal American, and I had a pipeline straight into the communist camp. It worked beautifully for months."

This pattern of hypnosis sounds exactly like that of Oswald's in which he was hypnotized to perform with his supposed defection to the Soviet Union. Oswald signed his death warrant when he made the statement, "I am a Patsy." He made this statement after his arrest and with it, failed the test as a Manchurian Candidate for which he had been programmed. The people in control knew he could never be left to live and tell what he knew, so he had to be eliminated. Jack Ruby was brought in and his mission was to eliminate

Oswald. Of course, this may have always been part of the master plan.

On April 16, 1953, Dr. Albert Hofmann made an incredible discovery. He accidentally took the first trip on Lysergic Acid Diethylamide (LSD) through the absorption of the substance through his hands while working in his laboratory. LSD is an offshoot of ergot, a fungus that plagues rye. While Hofmann was conducting his experiments with LSD, a few hundred miles away the Gestapo and S.S. were conducting their own experiments. They were also using the drug mescaline which is very similar to LSD in that users typically experience visual hallucinations and radically altered states of consciousness. The Gestapo was trying to discover if mescaline could be used to control unwilling people. Jews, Russians, and gypsies were used in the Gestapo experiments as they were deemed expendable and represented very little value. Many of these experiments took place in the Dachau concentration camp. These Nazi and Gestapo scientists are the same individuals who fled from Germany to South America in Operation Paperclip and ended up in the newly formed American Office of Strategic Service (OSS) intelligence program. These scientists brought with them records of these horrendous experiments.

Thomas Powers, author of *The Man Who Kept Secrets*, wrote the introduction to John Marks' book, *The Search for the Manchurian Candidate*. Powers wrote,

> "when clandestine operator's dream of the philosopher's stone, it's a surefire, no-fail, all-weather, inconspicuous device for the control of agents they have in mind –a "magic bullet" to make agents putty in their hands." Of course, there is no such thing. Agent-running is an art, not a science. But from its beginning in 1947, the Central Intelligence Agency has done more than simply dream of a magic bullet; it has spent millions of dollars on a major program of research to find drugs or other

esoteric methods to bring ordinary people, willing and unwilling alike, under complete control, to act, to talk, to reveal the most precious secrets, even to forget on command. Leading doctors and scientists were recruited to run many of these experiments, major institutions agreed to sponsor them, and some of the results were substantial. The CIA played a gigantic role in the development and study of psychoactive drugs just as the National Security Agency's code-breakers did in the development of computer software systems.

Dr. Louis Jolyon West performed LSD work for the CIA, and became famous, quite possibly even notorious and as some would say, because of his treatment of Oswald's assassin Jack Ruby. Nobody can explain why a CIA physician and Oklahoma resident was called in to treat Ruby in Dallas. I find it puzzling that in a city that had an ample supply of physicians, why a CIA physician would have been summoned to treat him. Ruby died of a fast moving cancer shortly after Dr. West examined him and Ruby claimed that he had been injected with cancer cells by his physician.

The term Manchurian Candidate was coined by Richard Condon in his book published in 1959 by the same title. It was made into a very popular movie starring Frank Sinatra, Laurence Harvey, Janet Leigh, and Angela Lansbury. In the movie, Harvey plays the part of a brainwashed soldier returning from the Korean War where he was programmed by the communist Korean Government to kill the President of the United States. The enormous difference between Oswald and the Kennedy assassination and the movie is that Oswald did not carry out the actual shooting, but was placed in the compromising position of being a Patsy. Oswald obtained his job at the Texas School Book Depository a few weeks prior to the assassination, the parade route was changed, and the roof was removed from the Presidential limousine. In the case of the Kennedy assassination, a foreign government was not involved unless the supposed mole that James Angleton was always searching for was foreign and pulling Oswald's strings. Kennedy became a victim of his own government; an American coup d'état.

A more current version of the *Manchurian Candidate* movie was released in 2004 and starred actor Denzel Washington as the young veteran, Ben Marco. In this version, a computer chip had been placed in Marco's shoulder and was used to control his actions. This movie does not involve the military other than Marco's Army service where his mind control began. The movie involves espionage in corporate America, but by today's standards and Halliburton's involvement in government, it may, indeed, represent the military. I am reminded of the question, "does art mimic life, or does life mimic art?"

Timothy McVeigh, the man found guilty of bombing the Alfred P. Murrah Federal Building in Oklahoma City, accused the CIA of having placed a computer chip in his buttocks that controlled his actions. I do not think its possible that they could control his physical actions to make him commit the crime. However, I think they might have controlled McVeigh by tracking him via satellite as they arrested and detained him shortly after the bombing. He was arrested for speeding almost one hundred miles away from the bomb site, and incarcerated as a suspect. If you think of all the circumstances that could happen in a 100 mile radius on any given day, why arrest McVeigh? It was not necessary to control McVeigh, just have the ability to track him. As of 2004, all new and renewed passports have a tracking chip inserted within. Micro chips are being placed in pets and as I write, pet owners are finding their lost pets by satellite. The computer chip placed in McVeigh's buttocks seems like science fiction, but the idea does not seem so remote when one recalls Yale neurophysiologist Jose Delgado's stimo-ceiver experiments. Delgado's device was a miniature depth electrode that could receive and transmit electronic signals via FM radio frequency. The stimoceiver was placed within an individual's cranium and an operator could control a subject while the individual was allowed full freedom of movement. Delgado is perhaps most remembered by an experiment in which he controlled a charging bull via electrical brain stimulation. He stepped into the ring with an angry bull that had been implanted with a stimoceiver and when it charged, Delgado stopped its attack by merely pressing a button on a black box. This demonstration took place in 1953; think of what progress as been made since, especially in advancements in micro-technology. In Oswald's case it was not necessary that he be followed, but placed in a particular location where he could be found and arrested.

A theory exists that suggests that Oswald had an electrode implanted in his brain during a hospital stay while undergoing an adenoid operation when he was in Minsk, Russia. I view this as disinformation used to confuse and mislead a person in understanding the true story of Oswald's peculiar behavior. The theory instills doubt and confuses the true story of the CIA using hypnosis along with LSD on young unsuspecting Marines at the Atsugi Naval Air Station in Japan during the time Oswald was stationed there. In the book *We Were Controlled,* authors Lincoln Lawrence and Kent Thomas claim that Oswald and Jack Ruby were controlled by Radio Hypnotic Intracerebral Control (RHIC) and Electronic Dissolution of Memory (EDOM). Both Oswald and I were removed from our units and placed on general duty before leaving Atsugi. This gave the MKULTRA an opportunity to program or work on us without being hampered. The Marine Corps is culpable in the deliberate abuse of Oswald and me, as they would have had to release us from our job responsibilities thereby enabling the MKULTRA ample time to program us.

Let us fast forward to 2006, the following is an article that appeared the March 1 edition of *The Nation*, a Thai newspaper.

SCIENTISTS PUT ID CHIP IN TOOTH:

It is the ID card you will never lose or forget to carry with you unless your teeth fall out. Scientists have implanted an ID chip into a tooth to show how detailed personal information can be stored.

The scientists say the tooth chip will be useful to forensic scientists trying to identify bodies after natural disasters and terrorist attacks with numerous victims. They say it will also have advantage over a simple identity card.

"You put your ID card in your pocket, we put it in a tooth," said Patrick Thevissen, a forensic odontologist at the Catholic University of Leuvenin in Belgium. The ID chip can carry information including a person's name, nationality, and date of birth, gender and national ID code and can be read after death.

The idea came about because of the difficulty and expense of identifying victims of disasters from dental records. Trying to identify bodies after the Asian tsunami for example, relied heavily on forensics. But it was difficult and time-consuming; particularly when teeth had been badly damaged or when dental records were not available.

Thevissen and his colleagues told the annual meeting of the American Academy of Forensic Sciences in Seattle they had adapted an electronic identification tag which veterinarians injected routinely into animals. Similar radio frequency identification (RFID) tags are used by retailers to track stock. The tags, the size of a grain of rice, use the power from a radio pulse emitted by an electronic reader to send out a code which can be picked up. This code can be linked to a data-base containing a person's details or, as Thevissen suggests, spell out simple information directly.

Guy Poelman, a member of the team, has tested RFID tags in lab; he drilled a hole into a tooth and inserted the chip as he would a filling. It withstood normal biting forces and worked after being heated to 450 degrees Celsius and cooled. But repeated expansion and contraction of the tooth due to heating and cooling -for example from hot drinks- is a problem. Poelman wants to modify the design to include an insulating layer. The advantage of the tag, he said is that it will allow swift identification of a decomposed body.

When you put all identification data in one place in the body there can be no mistakes. You have an immediate identification, said Thevissen. Teeth are particularly hardy and can survive for hundreds of thousands of years. Many extinct primates, for example are known only from tooth fossil. "We want to store it in the tooth because it's the strongest and longed lived body part."

As I write this book, there is a charge that the United States government, or certain people within, sold out our national security through greed. A small company by the name of Inslaw Inc. developed a software program which would help attorneys and large city districts keep track of their criminal prosecutors' caseloads. The software program was titled Prosecutor's Management Information System (PROMIS). In 1982, Inslaw won a significant Justice Department contract to implement the system on a nationwide basis. This program would allow prosecutors to locate defendants and witnesses, track movements, and monitor current investigations. Inslaw also developed privately owned enhancements to RROMIS and had guarantee of proprietary rights to the enhanced version. The government stole this new enhanced PROMIS software program (or by a term the military is fond of using, a midnight requisition). The government did not pay Inslaw for the program which forced it into bankruptcy. Inslaw has been in an endless fight with the Justice Department to recover their loss.

It is believed that Osama bin Laden may have access to the U.S. computer tracking software program that enabled the terrorists to monitor our intelligence-gathering efforts and financial transactions. Former high ranking government officials have been implicated in this theft, and the beat goes on.

In the United States, a person is on camera almost everyday, everywhere. The cameras are at intersections, parking lots, all security locations, grocery stores, gas stations, banks, and not to mention satellite, the ultimate camera. Along with camera monitoring, there is also monitoring of paper and electronic transactions, credit cards, cell phones, global positioning systems, and the wireless network, to name a few. The old-fashioned trail is still in place and is controlled by super computers that now enhance such groups as the Social Security number system, your state driver's license, the federal and state tax system, and your military, dental, and hospital records. If you have been issued a passport later than 2004, it contains an imbedded computer chip that can be scanned at airports, borders, etc. The chip contains records of your travel profile and any other information that is deemed necessary which can be read immediately. Your educational transcripts as well as books you have checked out at your local library are also being monitored as well as your medical information, insurance files, and the most enormous information trail of all, the Internet. We are well beyond George Orwell's 1984.

In an earlier chapter I referred to the friendship between Frank Sinatra and President John F. Kennedy. Sinatra met Kennedy through his friend, the Hollywood actor Peter Lawford, who was Kennedy's brother-in-law. I return to this subject as Frank Sinatra was known to have mob connections. President Kenney shared a girl-friend by the name of Judith Exner with Chicago mob boss Sam Giancana and Exner testified that she carried messages between Kennedy and Giancana. It has been said that Giancana was responsible in delivering the State of Illinois to Kennedy in the presidential election against Republican candidate Richard Nixon. This influence or help was enough to help John F. Kennedy get elected into office.

Interestingly, Frank Sinatra purchased the movie rights of the original *Manchurian Candidate*, and kept it off the market for more than 30 years. Sinatra introduced Kennedy to actress Marilyn Monroe with whom Kennedy had an extramarital affair. Sinatra was banned from the White House by President Kennedy and years later Sinatra became friends with Richard Nixon who had lost the presidential election to Kennedy. Years after the Kennedy assassination, Sinatra became a Republican and was welcomed by President Nixon to once again visit the White House.

Dr. Sidney Gottlieb was given power over the mind control program, and the covert use of biological and chemical materials within the MKULTRA. In the fall of 1953 at Fort Detrick in Frederick, MD, Gottlieb tested LSD on some unwitting scientists from the Army Chemical Corp Special Operations Division. This was done against direct orders prohibiting LSD testing without participant permission. In 1973, when Dr. Gottlieb retired from the CIA, he appealed to Director Richard Helms and asked that all of his program records be destroyed. Helms destroyed the files along with some of his personal files. Not discovered nor destroyed were approximately 150 boxes that have provided the information that we now use to understand what took place during the mind control experiments within the MKULTRA.

Prior to the MKULTRA's origination in 1950 was the CIA's human behavior program operating under the code name of BLUEBIRD, later to be known as ARTICHOKE. Outside the Atsugi Naval Air Station during the time Oswald and I were stationed there, flourished a bar by the name of The Bluebird. It was frequented by the personal that worked with the MKULTRA including Oswald and myself and many other unwitting Marines. It is said the MKULTRA played their mind and drug games at the Bluebird Bar. Do you think the name of this bar was just a mere coincidence? The mind control experiments were also interwoven with radiation experiments and research on chemical and biological weapons. I was also used as a guinea pig in the radiation experiments in the Mojave Desert during the atomic bomb testing detonations. Prisoners in Washington and Oregon State were paid to have their testicles irradiated. These prisoners received $5 a month for this experiment.

The MKULTRA programs were motivated by Russia, China, and North Korea's use of mind control techniques. Three months after the director approved BLUEBIRD, the first team of controllers traveled to Japan with hopes of trying behavioral techniques on human subjects, probably persons suspected of being double agents. Three men arrived in Tokyo in July of 1950, a month after the start of the Korean War. These programs first began in 1947 as a Navy program under the code name of CHATTER. CIA Director Roscoe H. Hillenkoetter used unapproved funds to pay for these most sensitive programs. ARTICHOKE lasted just a little over two years before most of the behavioral work went to another CIA unit called the Technical Services Staff (TSS). ARTICHOKE spent considerable work trying to create hypnotic couriers known as Manchurian Candidates. The BLUEBIRD and ARTICHOKE materials that were discovered through the Freedom of Information Act established conclusively that fully operational Manchurian Candidates were created. These unknowing couriers were tested by physicians with top-secret clearance employed by the CIA.

The program has used other titles such as CASTIGATE when it used truth serum on human guinea pigs in Germany. While it was under the title of CHATTER, Professor G. Richard Wendt was chairman of the Psychology Department at the University of Rochester. He was a part-time Navy contractor who worked under a Dr. Thompson's supervision. Wendt accepted the request of CHATTER to weaken and eliminate the free will in subjects. The Navy began this highly classified project in 1947 with the hope of developing a truth serum that would force people to reveal their innermost secrets. During the summer of 1952, professor Wendt announced that he had found a concoction so special that it would be the answer to the truth serum problem. Dr. Thompson recalled he thought it would be a good idea to call the Agency, thinking they may have a subject with something to tell. Wendt became adamant, and said he would not tell anyone in the Navy or the CIA what his serum contained. He also stated that he would only do a demonstration, of course neither the CHATTER nor ARTICHOKE units could resist this offer. The Navy had no source of subjects for terminal experiments but the CIA agreed to furnish the human guinea pigs in Germany. Introducing amnesia was a very important goal of ARTICHOKE. It was said that from the greater the amnesia produced, the more effective were the results. It was obvious that if a victim remembers a treatment it would stop being a closely guarded secret. If somebody did remember the treatment, they were held in foreign prisons for a long period of time (or in Oswald's case "The Patsy" is eliminated). In numerous cases, ARTICHOKE team members claimed success in making their subjects forget. It was stated that short of cutting a subject's throat, true amnesia cannot be guaranteed. As early as 1950, the Agency had put out a contract to a private researcher to find a memory-destroying drug, but it was apparently to no avail.

In 1953, the CIA authorized MKULTRA to perform research using hypnosis for interrogation and to create torture-proof couriers by implanting memories that could only be retrieved with a prearranged signal. It also tried to get subjects to kill while under hypnosis. The hypnotic state was later enhanced by using drugs such as LSD on thousands of unknowing subjects. For 10 years the MKULTRA had been searching for interrogation drugs and a truth serum. LSD became the drug they used most along with other drugs such as caffeine, mescaline, barbiturates, peyote, and marijuana. This causes me to remember a line from the musical Hair: LSD-LBJ-FBI-CIA.

The later programs of the MKULTRA also tested radiation, electric shocks, electrode implants, microwaves, ultrasound, and other drugs on hundreds of unwitting human guinea pigs including hundreds of prisoners at Vacaville State Prison in California.

According to congressional investigators, the Air Force conducted experiments with LSD at the University of Minnesota as part of a Cold War era research program. The research was conducted between the years 1956 and 1971 and also included subjects from Duke University, Baylor University, New York University, and the University of Missouri. According to the General Accounting Office, approximately 100 people received LSD during the experiments. The CIA was so fascinated with the effects of LSD that it tried to corner the world market on the substance and for many years, it was the main source of LSD in the United States. A great deal of the drug came from NAS Atsugi. The scientists finally dismissed LSD as being too unpredictable. At the time, Major General William M. Creasy, chief officer of the Army Chemical Corps, felt that psychoactive chemicals such as LSD would be the weapons of the future. He felt that spiking a city's water supply with the drug and then taking over would be much more humane than firebombing a city. "I do not contend," he told *This Week* magazine in May of 1959, "that driving people crazy even for a few hours is a pleasant prospect. Warfare is never pleasant; but would you rather be temporarily deranged by a chemical agent, or burned alive?" Not to be outdone by the CIA, the Army Chemical Corp. came up with a drug called 3-quinuclidinyl benzilate or BZ. It was known as a super hallucinogen that could affect a person for three days. Its symptoms were headaches, giddiness, disorientation, auditory and visual hallucinations, and maniacal behavior. Some symptoms were known to persist up to six weeks. Some 2,800 soldiers were exposed to BZ, most of them knowingly.

This research also included spraying of zinc cadmium sulfide, a possible carcinogen, on approximately 239 American cities. This estimate was based on the number of cities in the flight path of the planes. In addition to spraying other cities that included Minneapolis and St. Louis, the Army sprayed chemicals over wide areas of the central and eastern United States. One flight went from South Dakota to International Falls, MN. Others went from Toledo, OH, to Abilene, TX, and from Detroit to Kansas. Millions of Americans were unwittingly exposed to these chemicals during these series of tests.

In 1959, author Aldous Huxley said, "It seems to me perfectly in the cards that there will be within the next generation or so a pharmacological method of making people love the servitude, and producing . . . a kind of painless concentration camp for entire societies so that people will in fact have their liberties taken away from them but will rather enjoy it, because they will be distracted from any desire to rebel by propaganda, brainwashing., or brainwashing enhanced by pharmacological methods." Even as I write this book the newly formed Homeland Security Act is delving into and restricting our freedoms guised by the idea that we are being protected from terrorism.

The MKULTRA did not drop their mind control program at Atsugi Naval Air Station, but followed Oswald and I back to the United States. It was said that the Military Language School in Monterey, CA, had a method of teaching foreign languages subliminally. Oswald was said to have been sent to this school where he was taught the Russian language in which to prepare him for his defection to the Soviet Union one month after his hardship discharge. During this time, I was stationed at Treasure Island in San

Francisco upon returning from the Far East and was in the processing-out program awaiting my discharge from the Marine Corps. My friend Robert's hometown was Monterey so on a weekend pass I traveled with him to visit the city. It was not until many years later did I realize this was an entire missing weekend for me, and that I was controlled, and possibly spent time at the Monterey Military Language School.

Since the origin of the MKULTRA there have been many people suspected of having been controlled by the various units of the organization. Candy Jones, a famous American fashion model, maintains she was used as a human guinea pig in a CIA mind control experiment. Donald Bain, in his book *The Control of Candy Jones* states that Jones led a secret life as a Manchurian Candidate for U.S. intelligence services during the Cold War. Candy was born Jessica Wilcox in Atlantic City, NJ, in 1925. Jessica's father deserted her family, and her mother has been described as puritanical and did not allow her daughter to socialize with other children. Thus, Jessica created imaginary friends, one of which was called Arlene. Arlene's character was the opposite of Jessica's and eventually became to be seen as a split in the girl's personality.

In 1941 she won the title of Miss Atlantic City and became one of America's most famous models and permitted her to tour with the United States Service organization (USO) in the South Pacific. It was at this time that she changed her name. Candy was first introduced into the spy world after a divorce left her with three children to support and deeply in debt. It was during this time that she met a retired Army General she knew from her travels with the USO, and was soon after approached by an FBI agent who offered her payment for the use of her office a government agency mail drop.

Candy Jones' presumed adventures in a government mind control program are viewed with skepticism by the general public and today are regarded as part of conspiracy lore. However, the Rockefeller Commission, created by President Gerald Ford to study CIA abuses within the United States, revealed in its 1975 report that the CIA did, in fact, test behavior influencing drugs on unsuspecting citizens.

Candy was introduced to a doctor by the name of Gilbert Jensen who worked for the CIA, in Oakland, CA. Dr. Jensen asked Candy if she would care to learn more, and earn money by getting more deeply involved in the intelligence field. Candy needed the money and accepted the position. Dr. Jensen performed hypnosis on Candy, and discovered a second personality by the name of Arlene. Dr. Jensen used this new personality to the advantage of the CIA and turned Candy into a virtual zombie.

Candy was sent to military bases, training centers, and secret medical facilities all over the United States. She was studied, trained for combat situations, learned different types of covert operations, the use of explosives, hand to hand combat fighting, also the use of disguise, and communications. Candy was also taught how to kill with her bare hands, conditioned to resist pain, and shown how to counter interrogation techniques. Dr. Jensen was so proud of Candy he would take her to military bases and display her as an example of narco-hypnotic success. She was also sent to Taiwan on test missions delivering envelopes and while there, was tortured with electric rods to see if she would crack; she remained steadfast and did not.

On one occasion Candy performed at CIA headquarters in Langley, VA, before a group of 24 doctors. Jensen wanted to demonstrate that Candy's training was so thorough that she would possibly kill herself upon command. To demonstrate his total control over her, Dr. Jensen placed a lit candle inside Candy's vagina. This is just one example of some of the sexual abuse she suffered in her hypnotic state. Unfortunately, sexual abuse was not a new practice for the CIA. It is disturbing to know that the MKULTRA operated "Safe

Houses" in Greenwich Village and San Francisco where unsuspecting persons were lured and hallucinogenic drugs were used. This occurred while agents sat on the other side of two-way mirrors and monitored unsuspecting victims performing sexual acts and gauged their reactions to the drugs given to them.

Other well-known possible CIA controlled persons include Chuck Barris, producer and host of the popular 1970s The Gong Show. Barris authored *Confessions of a Dangerous Mind* in which he claimed to have been a CIA assassin. He followed this with 2004 sequel titled *Bad Grass Never Dies*. Other individuals who may have been controlled by the CIA are John Lennon's assassin, Mark David Chapman; James Earl Ray who assassinated Dr. Martin Luther King Jr.; John Hinckley who attempted to assassinate President Ronald Reagan; Sirhan Sirhan the assassin of Senator Robert Kennedy; Arthur Bremer, the attempted assassination of Governor George Corley Wallace; Candy Jones; and Lee Harvey Oswald. The list goes on and on. I also question the behavior of Charles Whitman the young man who was a model Marine and former Eagle Scout, who committed the shootings at the Texas Tower on the University of Texas campus. The autopsy supposedly showed a small tumor that questionably caused this unusual behavior on this formerly model Marine. Whitman was a Marine - was he somehow also exposed to the MKULTRA program? I also question if Charles Whitman spent time at Atsugi as he was stationed with the Marine Corps in Japan.

This type of conduct on the part of the CIA had nothing to do with fighting communism, it was just perverse experimentation. Winston Churchill called this type of experimentation, "perverted science" operating within an old style intelligence regime. The CIA disclaimer had stated its mind control program experiments were strictly a defensive response to the Chinese brainwashing of prisoner's of war during the Korean War. The truth is that the CIA saw mind control as a way to create torture-proof couriers and accomplished this by implanting memories that could only be retrieved with a prearranged signal.

The obituary of Stanley Gottlieb, the father of the mind control experiments, appeared in the March 1999 issue of *Time Magazine.*

> Died: Stanley Gottlieb, 80, eccentric chemist, who ran some of the CIA's most shadowy operations, including the agency's infamous mind-control experiments, of the 1950s and '60s; in Washington. Gottlieb once said the paucity of U.S. knowledge on the effect of drugs "posed a threat of the magnitude of national survival" to explain the existence of MKULTRA, a program that mandated dosing unsuspecting citizens with LSD.

You are in for a startling awakening if you think the mind control program died with Dulles, Angleton, and Gottlieb. In July of 1991, two inmates died at the Vacaville Medical Facility in Vacaville, CA. According to prison officials at the time, the two may have died as a result of medical treatment which was comprised of the use of mind control or behavior modification drugs. A deeper study into the deaths of the two inmates unraveled a mind-boggling tale of horror that had been part of the California penal history for many years, and caused a national protest years ago.

During the Reagan administration the top-secret program "Operation Sleeping Beauty" was created. Its intent was to explore the possibility of using electromagnetic waves to obstruct the functioning of the human brain and nervous system. What were they trying to accomplish with this program? Some program objectives included the derangement of a person's mind that would paralyze the capacity to reason and react, induce a fit of anger, create a state of panic, and to create a state of lethargy and apathy. Justification for the program included the belief that electromagnetic fields could be used for disrupting hostage takers. It could also be used to quell angry mobs by shooting them with electromagnetic waves which would cause the rioters to become sick. They also believed the weapon could be used on terrorists who may be imbedded in bunkers as the electromagnetic waves could penetrate walls.

When Richard Helms retired in 1973 he gave orders to destroy all CIA drug test records. He hoped that by destroying these records, all memory of the experiments and its victims would be lost forever. Of course, this did not happen and with the passing of the Freedom of Information Act, records keep surfacing. Richard Helms referred to these mind control experiments as harmless research programs.

One of the goals of the MKULTRA was to produce prolonged and indefinite amnesia so that once the agents were used; their memories could be erased, even on their death bed. I certainly do not recall everything that has taken place while I was under the control of the MKULTRA, but I do recall enough to expose the MKULTRA program, and their mind control of Lee Harvey Oswald and myself.

I am certain there are still many individuals who recall unusual circumstances during their military service, years in college, while incarcerated, or working in a capacity of importance, and especially those working in the intelligence field. Some individuals may vividly recall unusual circumstances although they may have never questioned the event, while others will recognize something unusual had transpired, but their memory remains fragmented. Some individuals may have a friend or relative who spoke of such a situation or memory. More research is necessary to identify these individuals.

A deep-seated anger persists in me and is directed towards those individuals responsible for having taken advantage of me when I was an 18-year old Marine. This program, that took advantage of young naive Marines, was developed and authorized by my own government. I consider this a rape of the mind - what gave these individuals or programs the right to use and exploit us? It disturbs me to know that this took place during the time I was honorably, and in good faith, serving my country.

Chapter Four

United States Marine Corps

One could not find a more perfect source than within the United States Marine Corps for potential mind controlled candidates. The subjects were young malleable men loaded with testosterone just starting out in life. They wanted to change the world and desired to be something special and to make a difference. Marilyn Monroe was quoted as saying a Marine was "an over sexed underpaid juvenile delinquent" which was probably not too far off the mark. The Marine Corps itself can be considered a type of mind control organization. However, this is necessary in order to construct the type of Marine that would not fail to perform under extreme and stressful combat conditions.

From the time a young man or woman gets off the bus at either Paris Island, NC, or the Marine Corps Recruit Depot in San Diego, CA, the indoctrination program begins. The future Marine is belittled and degraded, and in the past, was even physically abused. However, physical abuse was curbed to some extent after an incident in 1956, when a junior Drill instructor marched his assigned platoon into Ribbon Creek at Parris Island, SC, and six marines drowned.

In the Marines, recruit basic training is called boot camp. If a young recruit is fat, he will loose weight, and if he is underweight, he will gain weight. If the recruit is arrogant, he will be taught humility, and if he is weak and shy he will learn pride and strength. The Marine Corps builds men and leaders. Years after my term of service, when I worked in sales for the Prudential Insurance Company of America, I noted that the District Manager was an ex-Marine as well as were the four top salesmen. None of the other men in the agency had served in the Marine Corps. The Marine Corps attracts a certain type of individual that has the necessary character clay. The Marine Corps acts as a sculptor to complete the Marine. Basic training usually lasts from 12 to

16 weeks and a recruit learns how to handle different types of weapons, is given discipline, instructed in personal grooming, and learns pride, leadership, survivorship, courage, and how to work as part of a team.

The first few weeks of boot camp can be degrading as the recruit's individuality is removed by having his head shaved and being forced to wear utility uniforms. Recruits are belittled and treated as though they are too stupid to perform meaningless tasks without supervision. I remember that we were not even trusted with the care of our own footlocker key, and it was tied around our necks on a shoe string which we were not permitted to remove. A recruit's personality is also removed and replaced by one constructed by the Marine Corps. While you are in basic training you are known as a "shitbird" or any other offensive name that may humiliate you. The drill instructor is certain to exploit any unusual physical characteristic you may have. I was very thin, so I was called Bag-of-Bones. If you should happen to wear glasses, you would be known as "four eyes" or "Coke bottles." This humiliation is carried out to strip away individuality in order to construct a strong character and build pride, as well as to determine how much abuse a recruit can endure.

Toward the end of basic training, drill instructors' attitude change towards those recruits strong enough to have survived the abuse they have endured. At this time, recruits are issued dog tags (metal personal identification tags) which replace the shoe string and key around your neck. Although it is a small token, every marine takes pride in qualifying for something as insignificant as a dog tag. You are no longer called a "shitbird"; that term is replaced with "Hey You John Wayne" or "Hey Marine." You no longer dress in utilities, or working uniforms, but new green uniforms with barrack hats and shoes. Some Marines, who could afford it, would even purchase an expensive dress blue uniform.

When graduation day arrives, you realize you are now a Marine and a member of the world's most elite fighting force. You march "in parade or review" past bleachers filled with parents, friends, and girlfriends who made the trip to either Paris Island or San Diego to watch. I remember the chills that ran up my spine as I marched by the bleachers as the Marine Corps Hymn played. I was a full-fledged Marine, one of the few and the proud. I recall the large bold lettering written across headquarters office at the 5th Marines on Camp Pendleton. It read, "If, in future years men should ask you, what have you done? You can look at them proudly and say, I served with the 5th Marine Regiment United States Marine Corps."

It is astonishing to know that just a few months after my graduation, MKULTRA was on the scene. My personal service records had been controlled and agents had traveled to my small Wisconsin hometown to interview my parents, neighbors, school officials, teachers, and business leaders. From out of this information, my total personality profile was constructed. As a young, innocent, malleable, and willing young Marine, the addition of drugs, hypnosis, and sleep deprivation found me on my way to becoming a Manchurian Candidate.

Chapter Five

U-2 Spy Plane

On February 15, 1898, the battleship USS Main was sunk in a mysterious explosion in Havana Harbor. The Maine had arrived three weeks earlier and was docked in the harbor on a friendly mission to rescue Americans who had been caught in a Cuban uprising against Spanish rule. In an official investigation by the Navy, it was concluded that an external explosion was possibly caused by a detonated mine. This in turn, caused explosives within the Maine to detonate. Many theories abound, and one by Admiral Hyman G. Rickover suggested that one of the coal bunkers had exploded because of spontaneous combustion. In 1911, the Navy built cofferdams around the ship and removed its human remains before it was towed out to sea and scuttled. Unfortunately, we are still left with the mystery of what really happened to the USS Maine. However, there is no mystery regarding the ramifications of the sinking of this ship.

Theodore Roosevelt was Assistant Secretary of the Navy at the time, and accused the sinking to be "an act of dirty treachery brought about by the Spanish." William Randolph Hearst dispatched artist Frederic Hamilton to Cuba and his job was to draw pictures of the war. Hamilton reported back to Hearst that there was no war to which Hearst replied, "you furnish the pictures, I will furnish the war." Hearst published Hamilton's drawings which illustrated how Spanish saboteurs had attached a mine to the side of the USS Main. Because this information was printed in the New York Journal, the country erupted in righteous indignation and Congress, on April 25, 1898, declared war on Spain.

In the summer of 1898, Theodore Roosevelt left his position as Assistant Secretary of the Navy to join the 1st United States Volunteer Cavalry; later to be called the

"Rough Riders" by the American press. The group, made up of cowboys, Roosevelt's fellow Harvard polo players, and Native Americans, headed out for Cuba in 1898. It was there, at San Juan Hill, where Roosevelt and the Rough Riders made their famous stand. Because of the San Juan Hill battle, Roosevelt was nominated for the Congressional Medal of Honor which vaulted him into the seat of U. S. President.

There has been an ongoing controversy as to whether President Franklin D. Roosevelt had prior warning of the Japanese attack on Pearl Harbor which thrust the United States into World War II. Lies over the bombing in the Gulf of Tonkin lead to the Vietnam War, and we are currently at war with Iraq because of lies told regarding the 9/11 terrorist attacks on U.S. soil. It has been proven that Iraq did not have weapons of mass destruction, nor did the terrorists originate in Iraq. It is apparent that the truth did not matter as President George W. Bush and his administration only needed an excuse to invade Iraq; and that is what they did. After it was proven that no weapons of mass destruction existed, the Bush administration merely changed its objective to the spread of democracy in Iraq. The format for war and invasion never seems to change. Just as the lies regarding assassinations in the United States never seem to change; it seems as though it is always the lone nut. Granted some assassins are, but to group them together as lone nuts is disinformation. Yes, some are unbalanced, but let us start telling the truth with regards to those that were not lone nuts.

Other well-known lone-nuts and their intended victims include John Wilkes Booth (Abraham Lincoln), Sirhan Bishara Sirhan (Robert F. Kennedy), Mark David Chapman (John Lennon), James Earl Ray (Martin Luther King, Jr.), John W. Hinckley (attempted assassination on President Ronald Reagan), Lynette "Squeaky" Fromme (attempted assassination on President Gerald R. Ford), Arthur H. Bremmer (attempted assassination on George C. Wallace, Jr.).

Let us fast forward from the San Juan Hill battle to May 1, 1960, when Francis Gary Powers was shot down in a U-2 spy plane over the Soviet Union. At the time, President Eisenhower was attending the Paris summit with Russian Premier Nikita Khrushchev where the focus of discussion was disarmament. After the U-2 was shot down, Eisenhower refused to apologize and Khrushchev stormed out of the Summit after criticizing United States' spy activities. In his summit conference statement, Eisenhower stated that the U-2 activity represented no aggressive intent, but was to assure the safety of the U.S. against a surprise attack.

The cold war continued, the military complex won and continued to manufacture their weapons of destruction. It was later maintained by the Russian government that a Surface-To-Air missile brought down the U-2 spy plane. Later, a pilot from a Russian Mig-19 said that he flew so close to the plane that it crashed. Colonel Powers said that he thought an explosion came from inside and believed the plane had been sabotaged, which is a more likely answer than a Mig-19 flying at an altitude of 100,000 feet, or 20 miles in space. It must be acknowledged that many of the U-2 flights originated from Atsugi Naval Air Station in Japan. At the point in time that Colonel Powers was shot down, the Russians did not have Surface-To-Air missiles that would have been able to target a plane flying above radar detection, nor the ability to shoot it down at that elevation. In the sleeve of Colonel Power's flight suit, the CIA had placed a cyanide capsule along with instructions that in the event of capture, he should commit suicide. It was probably never expected that he would live through the explosion and parachute safely to the ground from such an elevation. Powers was interrogated by the Russians and subjected to a highly publicized trail in which he was found guilty and sentenced to 10 years in prison. He served just 21 months before he was part of a prisoner exchange that involved Rudolf Abel, a Russian spy being held in the U.S.

The U-2 spy plane project was part of Skunk Works, the name given to Lockheed Martin's Advanced Development Programs. The program also included the F-104 fighter jet; the world's first aircraft that could travel at the speed of Mach 2. Other programs included the SR-71 Blackbird and the F-117 Nighthawk Stealth Attack plane. The origin of the name Skunk Works is derived from the comic strip Li'l Abner. "Skunk Works" was a moon-shine still which produced Kickapoo Joy Juice made from old shoes and dead skunks. The original Lockheed facility was located down-wind from a foul-smelling plastics factory. In the 1960s, Lockheed changed the name to Skunk Works at the request of the comic's copyright holders. The Lockheed Martin Corporation holds registered trademarks to the name and skunk design.

I liken this story of the downing of the U-2 to the sinking of the USS Maine. The sinking of the Maine triggered the war with Spain; the downing of the U-2 kept the Cold War churning. Both of these incidents were caused by very mysterious and highly questionable circumstances.

At the time that the U-2 was shot down over Russia, there was a young Marine living in Russia who had once served at the Naval Air Station in Atsugi, Japan. He had been assigned to the air control tower and charted the U-2 spy plane. He had been given an early hardship discharge to return home to take care of his ailing mother. This young Marine's name was Lee Harvey Oswald, later to be charged by the Warren Commission as the lone assassin of President John F. Kennedy.

The CIA pointed their dirty finger at Oswald in the U-2 incident and stated that he had worked at the Control Tower at the Atsugi Naval Air Station. It was not mentioned that Colonel Power's flight had not originated out of Atsugi. Therefore, Oswald could not have known the flight plan. Also, it was well known that Oswald was in Moscow and all flight plans and codes had been changed according to Lt.

John Donavan. However, the CIA maintained that Oswald was privy to the altitudes, speed, charting, schedules, and destinations of the top-secret U-2 plane. This information is suspect as the U-2 did not fly on a regular schedule, and that the Power's downed U-2 did not originate from Atsugi. Also, the U-2 did not leave the air field without direct orders from President Eisenhower negating the possibility of Oswald knowing its schedule. Oswald supposedly had defected to Russia having been disenfranchised with the government in the United States, and applied for Russian citizenship. This was disinformation given by the CIA as Oswald never renounced his citizenship. He supposedly entered the Soviet Union under the guise that he had important information the Russians could use.

Lt. John E. Donovan, Oswald's commanding officer while he was stationed at the Marine Control Squadron One (MACS-1) in Atsugi, thought it very unusual that the Warren Commission did not ask him a single question regarding the spy plane. Donavan also stated that upon Oswald's known appearance in Moscow, all the codes, signals, flight paths, and information had been changed. Lt. Donavan also mentioned that he had long conversations with Oswald, which I think is highly unusual and suspect if you consider that Oswald had been portrayed as a "shitbird commie Marine." Throughout my time in the Marine Corps, I never had an officer sit down and have a conversation with me. Although my commanding officers always gave me proficiency grades and conduct evaluations, I doubt if any of them ever really knew who I was. Donavan had, in his possession, more information than he revealed to the Warren Commission. Donovan was Oswald's commanding officer during the time he was controlled by the MKULTRA and would have been privy to the fact that something irregular was taking place. Oswald would have needed permission, or at least knowledge on Lt. Donavan's part, to be absent during the necessary time it took for the MKULTRA to perform their transformation on him. It would have been impossible for a Marine with Oswald's job description and security clearance to be missing and do what he chose to do while either on or off duty. Not to mention that he publicly espoused Marxist and Communist doctrine while stationed at Atsugi. My commanding officer would have had to grant me permission, and would have also known that something was taking place, in order for me to be absent from my duty obligations. This would have allowed me to spend the large amount of time necessary to have been mind controlled and sent on various destinations as a courier. Atsugi was a closed base, and enlisted men below the rank of Sergeant, which Oswald and I were, qualified only for Cinderella liberty – to always return to the base by midnight.

While I was working at Atsugi's communications center, I would receive information when a U-2 Plane was about to land. I would jump into the communications Jeep with a fellow marine and drive out to the air strip. We would lie on our backs in the grass and stare into the sky to search for a glimpse of the U-2. I have no knowledge at what altitude the U-2 would enter our field of vision, but when we first observed it, the plane would appear as no more than a glint in the sky, no larger than a shiny grain of sand.

As previously mentioned, the U-2 spy plane was developed at what is now known as the Skunk Works Project at Groom Lake also now known as the mysterious Area 51. An Air Force Sergeant by the name of Robert G. Vinson told the unusual story of a military hop (free military plane ride) he had made to Colorado Springs, CO. He was told there were no planes flying in his direction, but at the last minute he was told that he could board a C54 that was going to Colorado Springs. The flight took him into Dallas on November 22, 1963, the day Kennedy was assassinated. Vinson thought it was unusual that the plane did not have military markings and had only a large circle of the world emblem painted on the tail. Vinson was the only passenger, and when they made a deviation into Dallas; the plane landed on a short sand strip approximately one and one half miles from downtown Dallas and the Dealey Plaza. Two men boarded the plane in Dallas and Vinson was certain that they were employees of the CIA. Later, after seeing Oswald's picture on television, he noted that one of the men had looked exactly like Lee Harvey Oswald. This story is told in the book *Flight from Dallas* by James P. Johnston and Jon Roe. Because of this flight, Vinson was transferred to work for the CIA at Nellis Air Force Base north of the Atomic Energy Commission's test site in Nevada. I relate this story here rather than in the MKULTRA chapter as Area 51, or Site 51, where Robert Vinson was assigned for his last years before retirement, is part of the MKULTRA program. While he was stationed at Nellis, he met the aforementioned Col. Francis Gary Powers, who also worked there upon his repatriation to America. Interestingly, Powers was part of the MKULTRA program before he was shot down over Russia, and returned to repatriate and again work for the program. The Nellis base adjoins the Nevada Nuclear Test site which was also a MKULTRA project that used humans as guinea pigs during the detonation of atomic bombs. During my basic training, I was used in these tests on an area called Frenchman's Flat, now part of Area 51.

It has been questioned as to whether a C-54 cargo plane could land on such a short landing strip as the one Robert Vinson had described. However, I don't question this as I remember watching a C-54 practice a maneuver known as "touch, and go" on the Atsugi airstrip. The plane landed and then took off immediately. I remember being surprised at the very short landing distance that was required for such a large plane to maneuver.

It is very intriguing to know that Col. Francis Gary Powers worked at Area 51 after his return from Russia, as did Robert Vinson after his ride to Dallas on November 22, 1963. Powers and Vinson both ended their careers back in the middle of the Central Intelligence Agency's MKULTRA program. The MKULTRA program was a program of total control.

Chapter Six
Atsugi U.S.M.C. Connection

As the saying goes, "there's no such thing as an ex-Marine," or "once a Marine always a Marine." Even though some of the following Marines served at different times, I will refer to all of them as ex-Marines. Most of the Marines included in this book served their tour of duty that covered an approximate seven year span that encompassed each other's military careers.

It is only fitting that as an ex-Marine and a product of the MKULTRA mind control program, I should be the individual to expose this plan that used unknowing and unwitting young Marines. It is as though the scorpion had just stung itself. It would be very interesting to know how far up the chain of command that knowledge of this dreadful program existed, and who gave permission to allow the program to go forward. There are far too many Marines involved in the Kennedy assassination for it to be a mere coincidence. Additionally, the Office of Naval Intelligence had to be an accomplice in this program in order for it to exist.

I question why there isn't a person or persons in government designated the responsibility of researching both old and new information regarding the assassination of President Kennedy. If there are people designated to accumulate propaganda information for Presidential libraries, why not designate someone to solve this crime? The case is not closed; it boggles my mind to think that a group of people could kill the President and have a story conjured up as improbable as the Warren Commission Report only to have the American public blindly accept its conclusions.

From the day of the assassination, I was aware that Oswald and I were both Marines and that we had served together in Atsugi, Japan. Because of this relationship, I followed the assassination case closely as it unfolded and began to notice unusual circumstances that developed. Many Marines began to materialize; all of whom had served at the Naval Air Station in Atsugi (NAS Atsugi) at the same point in time as Oswald and me. I also thought it remarkable that other Marines stationed at Atsugi in the midst of the MKULTRA program began to appear on the assassination suspect roster.

Lee Harvey Oswald was hired for his job at the Texas School Book Depository just days prior to the parade route having been changed to pass by the building in Dealey Plaza. And, through the insistence of Governor John Connelly, the protective bubble was taken off the limousine for the ride through Dallas.

In the years that followed the assassination, the investigation began to evolve, primarily because of the improbable verdict that was delivered by the Warren Commission. In this report, as well as reports delivered by the US Senate's Church Committee and the House Select Committee on Assassinations, the name of Roscoe White appeared again and again. The inclusion of White in the reports did not signal anything unusual in my own investigation until it was published that he had been a Marine. When I examined White's military service record, I was surprised to discover that he had been stationed at Atsugi during the time that Oswald and I were there. Additionally, White was a police officer on duty in Dealey Plaza at the time of President Kennedy's assassination. White had been hired by the Dallas Police Department just days prior to the assassination. Incredibly, we now have both Oswald and White who served at Atsugi and had been hired just prior to the assassination.

Kerry Thornley was one of the few ex-Marines to testify before the Warren Commission. He stated that he had a friendship with Oswald while they were stationed at Marine Corps Air Station El Toro (MCAS El Toro). That in itself is not as unusual as this was after Oswald had returned from

Atsugi. What is curious is that Thornley was also transferred to Atsugi and insisted that he had been used and controlled by the MKULTRA. At this point, the CIA and its MKULTRA program could control any of Thornley's testimony and thus substantiate the Oswald legend they had developed.

Noel Twyman in his book *Bloody Treason* devotes more than a chapter to Gerald Patrick Hemming. Hemming is another ex-Marine who had been stationed at NAS Atsugi. Hemming is a Soldier of Fortune type individual, and it was Hemming, not Oswald, who had visions of grandeur. The fact that Hemming still travels without worry of repercussion from the intelligence community, or self incrimination, makes me believe he is a disinformation junkie programmed by the MKULTRA. Hemming was never called to testify before the Warren Commission but did testify before the Church Committee and the House Select Committee on Assassinations. It is important to note that Oswald, White, Thornley, and Hemming, all ex-Marines, spent time at the same small airbase – NAS Atsugi.

Marines with NAS Atsugi, CIA, New Orleans, and Dallas Connections

- Lee Harvey Oswald was an ex-Marine who had been stationed at NAS Atsugi with CIA affiliations and who had lived in New Orleans and Dallas.

- Roscoe White was an ex-Marine who had been stationed at NAS Atsugi and who had lived in New Orleans and Dallas.

- Kerry Wendell Thornley was an ex-Marine had been stationed at NAS Atsugi with CIA affiliations and who had lived in New Orleans.

- Gerald Patrick Hemming was an ex-Marine who had been stationed at NAS Atsugi with CIA affiliations and who had lived in New Orleans and Dallas.

- Richard Nagell was an ex-Marine who had been stationed at NAS Atsugi and was a CIA intelligence officer who had lived in New Orleans.

- Frank Anthony Sturgis was also an ex-Marine and Army soldier who had been stationed at NAS Atsugi with CIA affiliations and who had lived in New Orleans and Dallas.

- Roger Craig was an ex-Army soldier who had been stationed in Japan and lived in Dallas. He was a police officer on duty in Dealey Plaza at the time of the assassination.

- Thomas Arthur Vallee was an ex-Marine who had been stationed at NAS Atsugi and had lived in Dallas. Valle had been implicated in a possible assassination attempt on President Kennedy to take place in Chicago.

- John Heindel was an ex-Marine from NAS Atsugi who had lived in New Orleans and whose name was used as an alias by both Oswald and Nagell.

- Malcolm E. "Mac" Wallace, an ex-Marine, was linked to various murders and is said by some to have been the real assassin of President Kennedy.

- Charles Whitman, the University of Texas sniper, was an ex-Marine who had been stationed in Japan and had lived in Texas. I include Whitman because of his Atsugi connection and the peculiar course his life took after he joined the Marine Corps; it was as if he had been a controlled person.

The city of New Orleans is included as a significant location and important enough that it illustrates a pattern that is suspicious in the Kennedy assassination case. As you can see, many Marines that had ties to the assassination also had lived in New Orleans. And, it is the city in which District Attorney James Garrison brought to trial New Orleans businessman Clay Shaw and implicated him in Kennedy's assassination. It is also where Oswald returned and worked for the Fair Play for Cuba Committee that helped the CIA establish him as a communist sympathizer and thereby created the Oswald legend.

While I researched the backgrounds of the aforementioned Marines, one obvious similarity began to surface; all had troubled childhoods. Was this a necessary requirement by MKULTRA in order to place them in their mind control program? Are children with dysfunctional childhoods easier to manipulate?

Roger Craig

Roger Craig was an ex-Army soldier who had been stationed in Japan and was a Dallas police officer on duty in Dealey Plaza at the time of Kenney's assignation. Much empathy should be awarded Craig and his difficult life. Born in Wisconsin in 1934, his family moved to Minnesota where he spent his childhood. When he was 12 years old, he ran away from home and worked as a farm-hand in various Midwestern states. In 1951, Craig joined the Army and served in Japan. Although he was not a Marine, he served in Japan during the same timeframe as Oswald, White, and Hemming.

Craig was a police officer with the Dallas Police Force November 22, 1963, the day of the Kennedy assassination. It was because of what Craig witnessed that changed his life forever. In Dealey Plaza, Craig heard shots and ran towards the Texas School Book Depository where he began interviewing witnesses. Approximately 15 minutes after the shots had been fired, he witnessed a man, who he positively identified as Oswald, exit from the rear of the Texas School Book Depository. Craig testified that Oswald slid down an embankment and climbed into a light green Nash Rambler station wagon that had traveled down Elm Street to pick him up. The station wagon was owned by Oswald's landlord, Ruth Paine. When later asked about the station wagon and who owned it, Oswald said, "That station wagon belongs to Mrs. Paine. Don't try to tie her into this. She had nothing to do with it."

Craig continued on into the building where he and fellow officers identified a rifle found in the supposed sniper's nest as a 7.65 German Mauser, and not the Mannlicher-Carcano they said Oswald owned. The Mannlicher-Carcano was later identified as the assassination weapon and it was confirmed that it was the same rifle that Oswald held in the now infamous photographs that with him dressed in black while brandishing two Marxist newspapers. He supposedly ordered the rifle from Klein's Sporting Goods in Chicago under the alias A. Hidell (it was later discovered that Hidell was a fellow ex-Marine from Atsugi).

Craig had been a model police officer who received four promotions and in 1960 was named "Officer of the Year" by the Dallas Traffic Commission. Because of his unbending position on what he had witnessed in Dealey Plaza, his life and career took a complete turn-around. Craig continued to insist that he saw Oswald get into the green Nash Rambler, and that the rifle he saw in the sniper's nest was a 7.65 German Mauser, and not the Mannlicher-Carcano. He held firm to his story, while everyone else yielded to the pressure applied to change their testimony. Craig noted that in 1964, he was interviewed by David Belin, a junior counsel for the Warren Commission. He later discovered that his testimony had been changed in 14 different places. Craig maintained throughout his life that what he saw that fateful day was just as he said it was.

Craig was fired from the Dallas police department and in 1967 was shot at while he walked across a parking lot; the bullet grazed his head. In 1973, he was badly injured when his car was forced off a mountain road. He later survived another shooting attempt made on his life in Waxahachie, Texas. And, the following year, Craig was seriously injured when his car engine exploded. He had told his friends that the Mafia had decided to kill him. Perhaps it was the CIA that decided to kill him? On May 15, 1975, Craig was found dead of a self-inflicted gunshot wound. If Roger Craig had not been a truly honorable man that maintained his testimony, he may still be alive today and able to enjoy his retirement years with his grandchildren.

Thomas Arthur Vallee

Most people are unaware that two other assassination attempts were planned on President Kennedy's life. One was scheduled to take place on November 2, 1963, in Chicago, just 20 days prior to the scheduled hit in Dallas. The second hit was to take place on November 18, 1963, in Miami just four days prior to the Dallas event.

The Chicago plot was thwarted by Abraham Bolden, the first African American Secret Service agent who had been hand-picked by President Kennedy to be part of the White House detail. Bolden spent only three months working directly for the President and was then transferred to Chicago. He claimed that in October of 1963, the Chicago office had received a teletype warning that an attempt would be made on President Kennedy's life. The warning stated that a hit squad consisting of four Cuban men, armed with high powered rifles and positioned atop high buildings, would assassinate the President. The Chicago plot was to be committed by an Oswald-type person and Atsugi Marine, Thomas Arthur Vallee. Vallee was a member of the John Birch Society; an organization dedicated to preserving and restoring freedom under the U.S. Constitution, and had been a vocal critic of Kennedy. He was arrested by the Secret Service in Chicago. At the time of his arrest, he was found to have an M-1 rifle, a hand gun, and 3,000 rounds of ammunition. It was reported that he had asked for time off from his employment on November 2, 1963. Vallee was released from jail on the evening of November 2 and was still considered to be a danger, but no word of this was forwarded to the Dallas Secret Service - the path to President Kennedy.

The Secret Service failed to notify the Dallas division and other law enforcement agencies about Vallee and also ignored a warning from Joseph Milteer, a far-right and racist political activist. On November 18, just four days prior to the arrival of President Kennedy in Dallas, Milteer gave detailed information on an impending assassination attempt on Kennedy's life to take place in Miami. Milteer detailed how the President would be assassinated by people with high powered rifles in tall buildings. Later when the Warren Commission convened, Abraham Bolden learned that this information was not being presented to the Commission. Bolden complained and was told to keep his mouth shut. Because he was a dutiful Secret Service agent, he took it upon himself to travel to Washington where he then contacted the Warren Commission Counsel. For some reason, Bolden was immediately arrested and taken back to Chicago where he was charged with having discussed a bribe with two known counterfeiters. Bolden was charged and found guilty of accepting the bribe and was sentenced, to six years in prison. Bolden tried to bring attention to his case, but consequently was placed in solitary confinement.

The Secret Service eventually admitted that the Chicago assassination threat did occur, but declined to explain the circumstances. Years later, because Bolden could not identify Vallee as a participant in the Chicago assassination threat, researchers concluded that Vallee had no part in the second assassination arrangement. I question this conclusion as coincidently, Vallee was an ex-Marine who served at NAS Atsugi. When it comes to the obvious Marine Corps Atsugi connection, the conclusion seems obvious and elementary that Vallee was, indeed, involved.

Frank Anthony Sturgis

Frank Anthony Sturgis was born Frank Anthony Fiorini, but later changed his name to take that of his stepfather. Sturgis was also known by the aliases Fred Frank Fiorini, Anthony Sturgis, Attila F. Sturgis, and Edward Joseph Hamilton. He enlisted in the Marines in 1942 and spent the greater part of his life employed by the CIA. He also had numerous ties to the mafia and was involved in activities in Florida that were run by Santo Trafficante, Jr., and the gangster Meyer Lansky. Interestingly, both mobsters ran several casinos in Cuba under the sanction of President Batista.

Sturgis also had ties to Cuba and he and Fidel Castro shared the same mistress, Marita Lorenz. In 1960, Sturgis and Lorenz were involved in a botched CIA assassination attempt on Castro. Sturgis was a member of Operation 40, a CIA undercover assassination operation created by President Eisenhower and led by Richard M. Nixon. Members were trained in terrorism, interrogation, and torture techniques, and it was believed that the group's primary focus was to kill Communists. It is also believed that Sturgis helped the CIA plan the Bay of Pigs invasion and was also involved in the "Pentagon Papers" break-in at the office of State Department official Daniel Ellsberg.

Sturgis' fellow Atsugi Marine, Kerry Thornley, testified before the Rockefeller Commission that while he lived in New Orleans, he had conversed with E. Howard Hunt about his plans to assassinate President Kennedy. Sturgis and Hunt were later linked as on the day of the assassination, three men were apprehended by the Dallas police behind the picket fence on the grassy knoll. The men were later released as they were believed to be railroad tramps. Newsweek Magazine published photographs of the men and two were believed to be Sturgis and Hunt in disguise. Sturgis never denied that he was one of the railroad tramps although he later maintained that Kennedy's assassination had been organized by Fidel Castro and Che Guevara and that Oswald had been a Cuban agent.

Sturgis' name shows up with surprising regularity and he was also involved in a trip to Mexico to obtain arms before the Kennedy assassination with fellow Atsugi Marines Gerald Patrick Hemming and Oswald (Oswald's double may have actually made the trip). Marita Lorenz also accompanied the men. In later testimony, Sturgis stated that he had never met Oswald, a statement that may be true as he may have known that Oswald's doppelganger was on the trip to Mexico, and not Oswald.

Roscoe White

When I examined Roscoe White's military service record, I was surprised to discover that he had been stationed at Atsugi during the time that Oswald and I were there. White was a Dallas police officer on duty at Dealey Plaza at the time of President Kennedy's assassination. He had been hired just days prior to the assassination and had allegedly written in his diary that he was the assassin positioned behind the picket fence on the grassy knoll in Dealey Plaza. Photographs of the grassy knoll area indicate that in the bushes there appears to be a person wearing a policeman's badge.

Years later, White's son, Ricky Don, claimed to have discovered his father's diary hidden in the family's attic. Ricky stated that his father had written the following incriminating statement. "I was Mandarin, the man behind the stockade fence who fired two shots. Lebanon was the man in the Book Depository who fired two shots. Saul was the man in the records building who fired two shots." Oswald had not been mentioned by name, but apparently he was the Patsy, and not one of the shooters. According to Ricky, his father made the fatal head shot that killed President Kennedy. Unfortunately, the naive Ricky trusted the intelligence community and made the mistake of handing over the diary to the FBI.

Like the disappearance of many key witnesses to the Kennedy assassination, the diary has also disappeared. It is interesting to note that with the finger directly pointed at the intelligence community in the death and possible cover-up of the assassination, the CIA accused Ricky of lying and questioned whether or not the diary had even existed. However, they failed to mention that White's wife, Geneva, had worked at the Carousel Club owned by Jack Ruby and that White had served with Oswald in the Marine Corps. The two had sailed on the USS Bexar to Japan and both had worked in the same MACS ONE squadron that handled the U-2 spy plane project which placed both of them within the grasp of the MKULTRA mind control program. Also, both men obtained employment in Dallas just weeks prior to the change to Kennedy's parade route that took it through Dealey Plaza and past the Texas School Book Depository.

The following article was written and published by George Haj in the August 7, 1990, issue of USA Today.

CIA: Latest JFK plot claim 'ludicrous'

CIA officials Monday rejected as 'ludicrous' a Dallas man's claim that his father was one of three CIA operatives who assassinated President John F. Kennedy.

During an earlier news conference, 29 year old Ricky White said his late father, Roscoe White, joined the Dallas Police Department so he could carry out the assassination.

White said Lee Harvey Oswald and police officer J.D. Tippit, who Oswald supposedly killed after the 1963 assassination, were "patsies." Oswald was a part of the conspiracy, while Tippit was uninvolved, White said.

He said much of his information came from his father's diary, but he could not produce the book. He suggested FBI agents had taken it. The FBI said that, in 1988, it received the same information as White divulged Monday but "determined that this information is not credible."

The CIA denied the claims. "These allegations – that this was done on CIA orders, that this guy worked for us and that the CIA had any role in the assassination of President Kennedy – are ludicrous," spokesman Mark Mansfield said.

Official investigations of the assassination concluded Lee Harvey Oswald acted alone. White's news conference was at the JFK Assassination Center in Dallas, a group that has pursued the idea of a conspiracy and cover-up. "We hope the (Texas) attorney general will reopen the case," said center director Larry Howard. "The federal government has done two investigations, but they haven't done it right yet."

Dozens of reporters covered the news conference, and Howard said later he "had 300 to 400 calls today. We've been on several news shows and Inside Edition is filming too. The response has been incredible."

White's theory has credence in the eyes of one man who investigated the assassination.

Former New Orleans prosecutor Jim Garrison still maintained the CIA was behind Kennedy's death. He tried New Orleans businessman Clay Shaw in 1969, but a jury rejected Garrison's claim that Shaw was part of a CIA plot.

"There is the possibility that this is valid because there are so many points where this kind of statement......usually veers off into unbelievably,"

Garrison said: "This statement continued to ring true."

But Woody Specht, and FBI agent who spent nine years assigned to the assassination case, said: "There's been so many claims like this in the last 27 years. You have to use good judgment here, especially from somebody who was what, two years old at the time?'

This last statement by former FBI special agent Woody Specht is typical of the "stinking thinking" that prevails and that the American public seems to accept. The fact that White's son was only two years old at the time of the assassination has no relevance to the fact that he found his father's diary that revealed the assassination information.

We know for certain that Roscoe White served with Oswald at NAS Atsugi and that his wife was employed by Oswald's assassin, Jack Ruby. Additionally, both White and Oswald were hired just weeks prior to the assassination that placed them in Dealey Plaza where the altered parade route would pass. The very route had been changed in the final hours that led up to the parade. I question why these facts have not been explained as they are not ludicrous.

White's wife Geneva maintained that he had written in his missing diary that he had been a contract man for the CIA. In the diary, he claimed that he had killed ten times and his hits included targets in Japan and the Philippines. White maintained this account throughout his life and according to his minister, on his death bed he asserted that the industrial accident that eventually killed him had been arranged by the CIA.

Joe West, a private investigator for Matsu Corporation said that after "seventeen months of searching for the truth, the whole truth, and nothing but the truth, the evidence that I've gathered concludes beyond any reasonable doubt that there was a firing squad in Dealey Plaza on November 22,

1963. Beyond a reasonable doubt, Roscoe Anthony White was one of the members of that firing squad."

It should be noted that Ricky Don White passed a polygraph test taken on November 26, 1990.

Gerald Patrick Hemming

Gerald Patrick Hemming is an enigma; he travels unobstructed within the United States and gives seminars and speeches about the assassination of President John F. Kennedy. One would think that if Hemming knew something pertinent about the assassination; his life would have been shortened just as the lives of many key witnesses had been shortened over the years following the assassination. Therefore, one can only assume that he is a disinformation junkie and an instrument in the cover-up, and the powers-that-be know he is harmless and reveals nothing of significance.

As previously mentioned, Hemming is a soldier-of-fortune type individual and allegedly was involved in many CIA-backed activities during the 50s, 60s, and 70s. CIA files show that his background is comparable to Oswald's. Hemming's security file (OS-429-229) was established at almost the same time as Oswald's (OS-351-164) and while Oswald's file was issued at the time of his defection for Russia, Hemming's file was issued when he was debriefed.

Much has been written about Hemming and his connections to Oswald and James Angleton. Hemming was also a Marine and was Oswald's sergeant at NAS Atsugi. Hemming made contact with Oswald when they both returned to California and admitted that he was the mystery man that Oswald met at the main gate at the MCAS El Toro. There has long been a question of who this mystery man may have been. In all of the speeches that I have heard or read, Hemming made no mention of the CIA and its MKULTRA program. This causes me to believe that he was unaware of the program, or was and continues to be a subject of the program. It is also possible that Hemming is aware of the program but continues to assist in the cover-up of its existence.

Hemming travels throughout the country and dupes people interested in the Kennedy assassination. He pretends that he is in control and that he may know something, but never reveals much of anything. Of course if he did, the intrigue would disappear. He would like us to accept that he was a Marine who could easily float around through the ranks of the Corps and travel freely even though he was an enlisted low-ranked non-commissioned Marine. Hemming insinuates he knows mafia members and wealthy influential people. He should stop his dog-and-pony-show, quit being part of the conspiracy theorist community, and reveal what he actually does know, if anything, regarding Kennedy's assassination.

However, there are a few interesting facts about Hemming. Apparently, he was on the infamous ride to Mexico with Oswald's double to obtain a shipment of fire arms. And he did have a relationship with Oswald while they were stationed in Atsugi. He was also involved in several nefarious operations such as the Bay of Pigs, Fidel Castro's takeover of Cuba, and the Intercontinental Penetration Force (Interpen) which he established in 1961.

Hemming was once asked why Oswald was sent to the Soviet Union and he replied that he was sent to be the fall guy when they dumped the U-2 Spy plane so they would get satellite financing. I believe this statement by Hemming to be factual and true. In a deposition to the House Select Committee on Assassination, Hemming testified that in 1963 he was offered money by New Orleans private detective and former FBI agent Guy Banister to kill President Kennedy. Interestingly, Hemming served as a consultant on the 1991 movie *JFK* and is listed in the credits.

Richard Case Nagell / Frank Olson

Richard Case Nagell, a decorated Korean War hero, resigned from the Army in 1959 because of a disability from injuries received in the war and a plane crash in which he was the only survivor. He had been left disfigured and had received permanent brain damage.

In 1958, while he served in Japan, he married Mitsuko Takahashi, a Japanese national. The couple had two children but their marriage ended in divorce when the children were very young. The divorce greatly disturbed Richard as this was the only real family he had ever known. Nagell's personal problems caused him a great deal of anxiety and were compounded by the fact that Mitsuko did not allow him to visit his children. At one point, Nagell checked himself into a hospital with a bullet wound and claimed that he had been shot by his wife. However, a doctor believed that the wound was self-inflicted.

Nagell's personal problems and his state of mind may result from where he was stationed at the time; he served dead center in the middle of the MKULTRA program in Atsugi. The pattern of Nagell's symptoms are very important, as he was conscious that he was progressively becoming unstable and felt himself regressing. He had lost a couple of jobs because he lacked the ability to concentrate and his nerves were overwrought which caused him to become even more unstable. He tried several times to obtain psychiatric treatment, but each time, he refused to cooperate when the request was granted.

Frank Olson was a scientist with the CIA in their MKULTRA program. He was suspected of being a security risk and while at a retreat with a group of CIA agents in November 1953, Sidney Gottlieb slipped a heavy dose of LSD into his drink that caused him to become agitated on the brink of being psychotic. A week later, Olson plunged to his death from the thirteenth floor of the Hotel Statler in New

York City. Olson's death was ruled a suicide until it was proven that he had been unwittingly drugged, struck on the head, and thrown from the window to his death. Olson had been in attendance at a meeting for a test project that involved the dispensing of mine-bending drugs to unsuspecting victims. The government went into a state of denial until the Olson family had his body exhumed 40 years after his death and the official autopsy report revealed traces of LSD. Olson's family threatened to sue the CIA but subsequently accepted a $750,000 settlement.

The "Honorable Man" and former member of the Warren Commission, Congressman Gerald Ford, became the FBI's stool pigeon during the Warren Commission proceedings. President Ford met with Olson's wife and children at the White House and apologized for his death; however, this came about only after the family threatened to sue the CIA (which the CIA could not allow to occur). President Ford told Olson's family members that the MKULTRA experiments were illegal and unconscionable. On the other hand, even though President Ford had to know the truth about Oswald, he never phoned Marina Oswald to apologize. The identical crime was perpetrated upon Oswald and the MKULTRA program that was responsible for Frank Olson's death, also took advantage of Oswald and placed him under their control. It has been very difficult for the government to keep a lid on the MKULTRA program and also to keep the truth covered about the Kennedy assassination. It was very essential to keep this MKULTRA program quiet.

There are many similarities in what happened to Oswald, Olson, Nagell, and also Charles Whitman, the ex-Marine who complained of the same type of mental anguish. Charles J. Whitman was the model ex-Marine that carried an arsenal of weapons to the top of the Tower on the University of Texas in Austin, where he began shooting people (see last section on Charles Whitman). I recall when I was stationed at Atsugi, at the same point in time as Oswald, Hemming, White, and Nagell, and how terrible I felt when the

MKULTRA was messing with my mind. My only way out had been to escape under a threat of death from a sentry guarding the area. I walked directly to the base Chaplin and sought the protection of the church.

When Oswald supposedly defected to Russia, there was much made about his state of mind when he made a feeble attempt to commit suicide. This was Oswald's cry for help as he attempted to escape from the MKULTRA's grasp – a program that he did not understand. It is doubtful that Oswald was ever again in control of his life after he arrived at Atsugi.

It is surprising to know that Oswald was stationed at the NAS Atsugi at the same time Nagell was stationed there as a military intelligence officer and contact agent for the CIA. Just as surprising is the fact that both were also together in Dallas, New Orleans, and Mexico City at the same point in time, along with Patrick Gerald Hemming.

Author Dick Russell wrote an excellent book entitled *The Man Who Knew Too Much* about Richard Nagell as the most important witness to the events that led up to JFK's assassination. Nagell maintains that on September 17, 1963, he tried to warn FBI Director J. Edgar Hoover and CIA operative Desmond Fitzgerald about the impending assassination. Nagell told them of an assassination plot to kill Kennedy that was to be carried out by Oswald and two exiled Cuban associates. Even if this story were not true, one has to question his actions, especially when we consider that he was stationed at Atsugi as an intelligence officer along with Oswald. Nagell was working as a double agent and had connections with the KGB in Russia, GRU intelligence services, Japanese Intelligence, and the CIA. In 1970, the Secret Service interviewed Marina Oswald for more than two hours in regards to Nagell. Apparently none of the notes have ever been made available to the public.

Nagell entered the State National Bank in El Paso, TX, on September 20, 1963, four weeks prior to JFK's assassination. He carried a .45 revolver and fired two shots into the wall. He then walked outside and immediately surrendered to the police. Because the State National Bank was federally insured it fell under the jurisdiction of the FBI. Nagell was interviewed by FBI agents and stated that he wanted to attract the attention of the court system in hopes that he would be granted permission to visit his children, which he had been denied through judicial proceedings. At a later interview, Nagell stated he had entered the bank with the sole purpose of getting psychiatric help and treatment and was not trying to rob the bank.

Nagell had said that during his military career he had worked for United States intelligence and the Russian Government when he was attached to the US Army Counter Intelligence Corps (CIC). The U.S. Government denies that he ever worked for them in an intelligence capacity, but they also denied that Oswald had any similar connections. Both Nagell and Oswald used the same alias of Alek Hidell. In 1973, when the CIA was planning to overthrow the government of Chile, they began a propaganda campaign to support Salvador Allende's political opponent. The CIA bragged that it had given 760 erroneous stories to news media around the world that discredited Allende. Do you think the CIA is capable of disinformation?

Nagell also stated that he knew of a young Trotskyite by the name of Harry L. Power from the San Antonio area that had a Mannlicher-Carcano rifle in an Indiana hotel room. This rifle was left there on the same day as the Kennedy assassination and is the same type that was supposedly used by Oswald in the assassination. This by itself does not mean much, but the fact that Nagell knew of this, and the fact that he was stationed with Oswald at Atsugi, brings much into question.

The honorable men on the Warren Commission knew of Nagell but did not call on him to testify. Later, when the United States House Select Committee on Assassinations investigated the Kennedy assassination, they also opted not to have Nagell testify. This makes one think that neither committee wanted to know something other than what they had already decided should be the outcome of their inquiry.

Kerry Wendell Thornley

I did not know fellow Marine Kerry Thornley personally, although we had much in common; we both knew that we were controlled by the MUKULTRA in Atsugi. Thornley and Oswald first met after Oswald's return from Atsugi and both served in the same radar operator unit at MCAS El Toro. Both shared many common interests and in particular, an avid interest in Marxist philosophy. It was from MCAS El Toro that Oswald received his hardship discharge to return home to assist his ailing mother. Instead, he defected to the Soviet Union. It was also from MCAS El Toro that Thornley and I shipped out for Atsugi. Thornley transferred to the very base that Oswald had just left which placed him in the middle of the MKULTRA program.

In 1962, Thornley finished a manuscript called *The Idle Warriors*, a work about an embittered Marine who defects to the Soviet Union. This book is often referred to as a portrait of Lee Harvey Oswald written before the assassination of President John F. Kennedy. It was because of this book that Thornley was called to testify before the Warren Commission in 1964. Thornley testified that Oswald was a Marxist and obsessed with Russian culture. Other Marines that testified before the Commission made no mention of Oswald's supposed Marxist obsessions.

I believe that Thornley was programmed because in his testimony he stated, "From my first press interview, I was cajoled, flattered, and coached to say just what the Warren Commission wanted to hear. For example, Clint Bolton appointed himself my manager and, just before the TV cameras went on said, "Kerry, this buddy of yours just killed their president; these people don't want to hear the good things about Oswald; they only want to hear the bad things."

New Orleans District Attorney Earling Carothers "Jim" Garrison believed there was a conspiracy to assassinate JFK and in January of 1968 subpoenaed Thornley to again appear before a grand jury. He was questioned about his relationship with Oswald and others who may have been connected to the assassination. Thornley denied that he had any contact with Oswald since 1959, and Garrison charged him with perjury. Thornley said he would not contest the point that he had given the Grand Jury disinformation regarding Oswald.

Thornley later claimed that had been a subject of the MKULTRA program but he was never taken seriously. I visited his website numerous times and felt that the MKULTRA had really messed him up. At the time of his death, he was working with journalist Sondra London to publish his previously completed manuscript called *The Dreadlock Recollections*. Ms. London has since published Thornley's account of his involvement in the conspiracy to assassinate John F. Kennedy.

John Renee Heindel

Kerry Thornley stated that he knew a Marine at MCAS El Toro that spoke Russian with Oswald. This man is believed to be John Rene Heindel who was known as "Hidell" to Oswald and other Marines. In a signed Affidavit for the President's Commission of the Assassination of President John F. Kennedy, executed in New Orleans, LA, on May 19, 1964, Heindel stated that he served in the United States Marine Corps from July 15, 1957, until July 15, 1961 and was stationed at NAS Atsugi with Oswald. He also stated that he was often referred to by the nickname "Hidell" and that it was possible that Oswald may have heard him being called by the name. Despite this fact, the Warren Report stated that there was no real "Hidell" and that the name was entirely invented by Oswald for his own purposes. Oswald used the alias "A. Hidell" to order the now infamous Mannlicher-Carcano assassination rifle and the post office box application to which it was delivered. He also frequently used the alias "Alek Hidell" and numerous documents in his possession, including a personal identification card, used some form of the alias "Hidell". Interestingly, Richard Case Nagell also claimed he used the alias of Alek Hidell. This is a great coincidence when you consider that Nagell was an intelligence officer at Atsugi. Heindel was living in New Orleans at the time of JFK's assassination and died there in 2000 at the age of 62.

Malcolm E. Wallace

Malcolm "Mac" E. Wallace enlisted in the United States Marine Corps in 1939, the same year Lee Harvey Oswald was born. Wallace does not qualify as an Atsugi Marine nor a Marine buddy of Oswald as Atsugi did not become a Naval Air Station until after World War II, when Oswald was an infant.

The connection with Oswald is that Wallace's fingerprints were found in the sixth floor sniper's nest in the Texas School Book Depository where Oswald was allegedly the lone assassin. His fingerprints have been officially identified by a 14 point match system. The prints were previously not identified, but had been stored in the national Archives. Doesn't this suggest a possible conspiracy?

Wallace has been linked to various murders, most notably the murder of Henry Marshall, a US Department of Agriculture Investigator. Allegedly, Marshall was close to linking Lyndon Johnson to the fraudulent activities of Billy Sol Estes, a businessman and convicted swindler. Under oath in 1984, Estes alleged that Vice President Lyndon B. Johnson ordered the killings of President Kennedy, Henry Marshall, and more than six other people. A grand jury in

1984 determined that Henry Marshall was murdered as a result of a conspiracy involving Vice President Lyndon Johnson, his aid Clifton Carter, and Mac Wallace. No charges were brought forth as all three men were now deceased. In 1952, Wallace had been convicted of first degree murder in the death of John Douglas Kinser. With a rigged jury and the help of two of Johnson's finest attorneys, Wallace got off with a five year suspended sentence.

Madeleine Brown, Johnson's longtime mistress, stated that Johnson had foreknowledge of the Kennedy assassination. On the eve of the assassination, Texas oilman Clint Murchison hosted a meeting in his Dallas home. In attendance were Johnson, FBI Director J. Edgar Hoover, and John McCloy, who was later to be selected by Johnson to serve on the Warren Commission. Madeline Brown stated that in the middle of November she had seen Johnson meeting at the family television station with Cliff Carter and Mac Wallace. Billy Sol Estes stated that Wallace was the group's assassin and it is also said that Mac Wallace had connections with the world of intelligence.

Wallace was killed in a single car automobile accident in Pittsburg, Texas, in 1971 at the age of 50.

Charles J. Whitman

It is with reluctance that I bring Charles J. Whitman into this book as he was not involved in the Kennedy assassination. I do this only because he served in the United States Marine Corps in Japan. I have tried in vain during the course of my research to locate whether a portion of Whitman's Marine service was at the MCAS in Atsugi or Iwakuni. Even if Whitman's records would indicate he was not stationed at Atsugi, it does not necessarily mean that he was not in the MKULTRA mind control program. Because Whitman was stationed in Japan, it would have been easy for the MKULTRA to have access to him.

Whitman was a model child, who, at age 6, had scored 138 on a Stanford-Binet IQ test. He was an alter boy, an accomplished pianist, and at age 12, was one of the youngest ever to qualify as an Eagle Scout. Whitman graduated with honors and at age 18, much to the disappointment of his father, enlisted in the United States Marine Corps. While enlisted, Whitman qualified as a Sharpshooter on the rifle range. Much has been made of this qualification just as much has been made of Oswald being a Marksman. In reality, Marksman is lowest of three ratings of rifle and other small arms proficiency and Sharpshooter is the second military grade of proficiency. The highest military grade of proficiency is that of Expert Rifleman. While on active duty in the Marine Corps Whitman was also awarded the Good Conduct and Marine Corps Expeditionary Medals and qualified for a scholarship under the Naval Enlisted Science Education Program.

Whitman enrolled in the mechanical engineering school at the University of Texas (UT) in August, 1962, and upon graduation, he was to have attended Officer Candidate School. While at UT, his academic performance became unacceptable and he was removed from the scholarship program and returned to active duty. While on active duty he loaned money for profit to fellow Marines, was charged with gambling, and was found to have weapons in the barracks. Whitman was court-martialed and reduced to the rank of Private. (While a Marine, Oswald was also charged with a weapons violation.) Once removed from their unit, and supposedly placed in the brig, the MKULTRA had all the time they needed to begin its mind control program on the unwitting Marine. In December 1964, Whitman was awarded an Honorable Discharge. He returned to civilian life and enrolled once again at UT, but this time in its architecture program. Without a scholarship, Whitman worked as a bill collector and as a bank teller at the Austin National Bank. He also volunteered as a scoutmaster for the 5th Austin Boy Scout Troup. While in college, Whitman became depressed and visited the campus psychiatrist and was prescribed both Dexedrine and Excedrin for his symptoms.

Shortly after midnight on the eve of the Tower shootings Whitman killed his mother and left a handwritten note that included the following text.

"I have just taken my mother's life. I am very upset over having done it. However, I feel that if there is a heaven she is definitely there now...I am truly sorry...Let there be no doubt in your mind that I loved this woman with all my heart.

After writing this note he returned home stabbed his wife Kathy while she slept. The following appeared in another note typed on July 31, 1966.

"I imagine it appears that I brutally killed both of my loved ones. I was only trying to do a quick thorough job."

"If my life insurance policy is valid, please see that all the worthless checks I wrote this weekend are made good. Please pay off my debts. I am 25 years old and have been financially independent. Donate the rest anonymously to a mental health foundation. Maybe research can prevent further tragedies of this type."

On the morning of August 1, 1966, Whitman entered the Bell Tower on the UT campus and carried an arsenal of weapons, ammunition, and personal supplies to the top. Over a period of 96 minutes, he killed 16 people, and wounded another 30. The siege ended when police officers Ramiro Martinez and Houston McCoy shot and killed Whitman.

An autopsy of Whitman's brain revealed a walnut-sized tumor located beneath the thalamus, which many believe caused his erratic behavior. As Whitman's friends and relatives needed closure, they clung to this analysis, but experts concurred this answer was questionable.

Even though Whitman was acting crazy and erratic, he also had a sense of responsibility for his actions. He left behind lengthy coherent suicide notes and understood that he was suffering from irrational urges, but did not understand how to react to those emotions. He began his suicide note with the following.

"I don't quite understand what it is that compels me to type this letter. Perhaps it is to leaves some vague reason for the actions I have recently performed. I don't really understand myself these days. I am supposed to be an average reasonable and intelligent young man. However, lately (I can't recall when it started) I have been a victim of many unusual and irrational thoughts."

Whitman asked that his brain be studied after he died and that his estate be donated to research similar types of mental illness. Poor Whitman most likely never knew he was possibly a guinea-pig in the MKULTRA mind control program. This would place him in the same category along with Richard Case Nagell, Frank Olson, Lee Harvey Oswald, and me.

Much speculation arose in the aftermath of this tragedy. President Lyndon Johnson immediately began to advocate gun control and Governor John B. Connally commissioned a panel to study exactly how the tragedy had taken place. Both men were riding in the parade caravan when JFK was assassinated. Were their decisions to further investigate the Whitman tragedy made because they thought it was necessary to continue to keep a lid on the MKULTRA program? The program was never discussed in any of the investigations and President Johnson and Governor Connally were part and parcel of the assassination cover-up which involved the MKULTRA.

Chapter Seven

Hawk, an Atsugi Marine

Hollywood typically portrays someone who has lost their memory as suddenly and miraculously awakening from their stupor and totally aware of their past. Because of this depiction, I have also been guilty of expecting this miracle to occur to me. In fact, many who suffer from memory loss have a difficult time regaining their memory and oftentimes, do not ever regain full memory. Unfortunately, I can recall only portions of what has taken place in my past, and cannot recall the total experience. I want to emphasize that to my knowledge, I have not regained any portion of my lost memory. The nearest I have approached to recalling a memory is the experience I describe in the following "Robert, an Atsugi Marine" chapter. I experienced chills and the hair stood up on my arms when Robert related the experience of how we witnessed a young man's murder by the Chinese Military in a rice paddy in Taiwan. In this book, the portions of my memory I write about were never lost and do not represent memory recovery.

However, my existing memories have become more vivid because of the selected segments that have been blocked by the MKULTRA control program. The missing segments of my memory made the process of writing this book much more difficult and took a considerable amount of time and concentration. The memory blocks have made it increasingly difficult to piece together the undamaged or buried segments. There was a time when I was totally unaware that anything extraordinary had taken place. Through reading and research I have been able to fill in most of the blanks thanks to many wonderful authors and researchers.

I returned to my home on Main Street in Viroqua, Wisconsin, in June of 1959. I recall my first evening home; I sat alone on the sidewalk steps well past midnight just relaxing and watching the cars pass by. I was troubled and was attempting to understand my life, which was totally separate from the one I had left three years before. At that moment, I could relate to Earnest Hemmingway's character of Nick Adams *Adventures of a Young Man*. I, like Nick, had been transformed from a naive boy who entered the United States Marine Corps, to a much more mature and seasoned young man after my military service. Having spent the last three years away, first in California and then in Japan, I found myself on the front steps of my home as though nothing had taken place. Everything was the same, except for me. I was totally unaware of what had actually taken place compliments of the CIA and their MKULTRA mind control program. In retrospect, I was oblivious as to what caused my angst. As the years passed by, my angst subsided and I fell back into the ways of my former self and life in a small rural town.

I believe I recall more vividly than most the answer to the classic question, "Where were you when President

Kennedy was shot?" I remember that I ran home when I heard of the assassination. My wife had asked me what was wrong and hurriedly I told her what had happened and turned on the television set where we sat together and watched the chilling events unfold. When the picture of the alleged assassin, Lee Harvey Oswald, flashed across the screen, I exclaimed," I know him." My wife gave me a doubtful look and questioned my sanity.

The weeks passed by and as information came forward, the so-called truth about the assassination became clearer. It was revealed that Lee Harvey Oswald was the name of the alleged assassin, and that he had served in the United States Marine Corps in Atsugi, Japan. I passionately followed the unfolding saga and I read the Warren Commission Report at the insistence of my brother Marvin. I became even more interested in the case after Mark Lane's book *Rush to Judgment* was published. At this time, I had not yet experienced my revelation of what had actually taken place at the Spook Base in Atsugi, Japan. My revelation occurred in the spring of 1983 when the computer industry was in its infancy. I was a representative for an insurance company based in Milwaukee, WI, and its sales director had requested that I meet him at the corporate office so that he could demonstrate the benefits a personal computer might have on my business. I was to meet him in the lobby of a Howard Johnson hotel in downtown Milwaukee. I arrived early and waited for him in a comfortable lobby chair. As I sat and gazed out the window, I observed the buildings across the street. Although I knew that I had never seen them before, they seemed very familiar to me. I searched my memory and it suddenly occurred to me where I had been with this similar view. The scene had reminded me of my view out a window several years earlier in a restaurant in Carmel, California, where I waited for Robert Two's return. This event had taken place during my missing weekend in Monterey. It was obvious that I had been controlled at that time as I had wanted to leave, but could not disobey my instructions to remain.

Previously, I had not given much thought about my time in Monterey, but as I waited in the lobby of the Howard Johnson hotel, everything that pertained to that odd weekend flooded back into my memory. It seemed peculiar that I had not recalled such an important occurrence and I had never before made a correlation between that weekend and any missing time from my memory. The manifestation of those lost memories mystified me as I was not able to recall how I arrived in Monterey, what had taken place during that weekend, nor how I had managed to return to the Naval Station at Treasure Island. Unfortunately, many of the missing memory segments remain a mystery but the portions I did recall, took on new significance. I became energized over the revelations and was bursting with anticipation to return home and search through my photos and memorabilia. What I found changed my life forever.

Shortly after my return home from the military, I met my former high school typing teacher who had taken on the new role of guidance counselor. He asked, "Hawk, what were you doing while you were in the military? We had government people here at the high school numerous times inquiring about you." My mother had also revealed that government men dressed in suits, not Marine Corps uniforms, had stopped by the house a couple of times to ask questions about me. I had cast off this information as a normal background check so that I could become certified for top-secret clearance. I now realize the interviews were necessary so that the CIA could construct my personality profile for their MKULTRA program. I had the top-secret clearance designation awarded to me while I was in Taiwan, but it currently does not exist on my military records. Interestingly, Oswald did not have an official top-secret designation in his military records, something that would have been required due to the nature of his job in the control tower at the NAS Atsugi in order to chart the flights of the top-secret U-2 spy plane.

If the government intended to use Oswald and me, as they did with the patsy description of Oswald, it would be necessary to depict Oswald as being a lone-nut assassin. How would it have appeared if it was known that the government had completed an extensive background check that qualified him for top-secret clearance, only to be contradicted by The Warren Commission's verification that depicted him as a dysfunctional lone-nut? The Commission would have had to grapple for a new answer as their original supposition of Oswald as a lone-nut assassin was totally incorrect.

Much has been made of Oswald's childhood, but very little of his time at Atsugi. Of course, the Warren Commission's outcome was predetermined. Its goal was to find Oswald guilty and direct all potential complicity away from the intelligence community. It was essential to add and omit evidence where necessary to absolve the real people that were guilty, and this task was achieved by those honorable men who were members of the Warren Commission.

I am still uncertain whether the MKULTRA had, or has, plans programmed for me.

Hawk on artillery placement outside Pingtung operated by Nationalist Chinese.

Chapter Eight

Robert, an Atsugi Marine

The CIA's MKULTRA program created a doppelganger, or double, of my friend Robert, just as they had with Lee Harvey Oswald. In Oswald's case it is understandable, as the doppelganger was used to create a legend that would incriminate Oswald as the assassin of President Kennedy and find him responsible for the downing of the U-2 spy plane. With my friend Robert, the use of a doppelganger is questionable since the MKULTRA would have had to been infiltrating a Marine Corps headquarters within its own government. Could it be that the MKULTRA was just playing espionage games, or were they actually gathering top-secret information? Another possibility may have been that the Chinese Communists had possibly infiltrated our headquarters and our MACS1 U-2 control squadron right under the nose of the MKULTRA.

To distinguish between the two Roberts, I will refer to the original as Robert and the second as Robert-2. I am certain that Robert and Oswald were unaware of their doubles. However, I am also certain that the doubles knew they were impersonating the originals. Possibly, they knew they were creating a legend, but did not understand their objectives and mission in order to give them plausible deniability. All men may have assumed they worked for the CIA and carried out the orders that they were programmed to perform; however, the originals performed their tasks while under control of the MKULTRA. There will be naysayers and pundits in regards to this Doppelganger hypothesis, but I assure you that what I write is true although it may seem incredible. I know; I was there.

Robert

The Doppelganger, Robert-2

I first met Robert at the 5th Marines at Camp Pendleton in California. I was attached to the Tactical Air Control Party (TACP) as a radio operator whose role in a combat situation would be as a forward observer who called in air strikes on the enemy position. This was my first duty station after completing basic training (boot camp) at the Marine Corps Recruit Depot in San Diego, CA. I had been stationed at Camp San Mateo, home of the 5th Marines, located on Camp Pendleton a short time before Robert was transferred into our section; we became close friends in the following days and years.

I was very intrigued by Robert; he seemed to have a great deal of knowledge on numerous subjects that were foreign to me. He grew up in Monterey, CA, while I was from a small rural community in WI. In the 1950's, these two cities were worlds apart, not only in distance, but in values, principles, and attitudes. While in basic training, I recall that our drill instructor forewarned our platoon about California girls and that they may appear more mature than their actual age. The drill instructor did not want us young Marines getting into trouble on a weekend pass by having a relationship with an under-age girl. He told us that the young people in California were just more advanced than the teenagers from the Midwest. I also attributed this characteristic to Robert, but in retrospect, it was more than just the difference between Midwest and West Coast values.

Robert told me he had been a member of a gang when he attended high school and showed me a devil's head tattoo on his shoulder that was its symbol. At that time, tattoos were rare and usually only seen on sailors or circus and carnival workers. Robert also knew the words to the Wiffenpoof song, the theme song for the extremely secret Skull and Bones society at Yale University. I mention this because so many former members of the Skull and Bones have gone on to become members of the CIA. For the past 50 years I have tried to understand who Robert really was and not just the individual he presented, or pretended to be.

To parody the television game show *To Tell the Truth*, "Will the real Robert please stand up?"

One rainy afternoon while we were sitting in the barracks chatting and shining our boots, Robert told me that a CID agent had been secretly placed among the men in our company. I didn't know what the letters meant and he said they stood for Civilian in Disguise. I accepted his answer but later found that the correct meaning of the acronym was Criminal Investigation Department, but at the time I didn't know the difference. I asked who he thought the agent was and he laughed and replied that he didn't know, but it could even possibly be him. In hindsight, I think that the CID agent may indeed have been Robert.

Robert was one of the few Marines I knew that was married while in the Corps. If a Marine was married, it was usually because he was older or a career Marine. He told me that he had married his high school sweetheart and that she and their two children lived in the Monterey area and that he visited them almost every weekend. I don't recall that he ever spent a weekend at Camp Pendleton, and he told me that he would hitch-hike the length of the state to return home to see his wife and children in Northern California. According to Marine Corps regulations, this distance was well beyond that allowed for a weekend pass. The distance he traveled every weekend was approximately 500 miles and I can't imagine at what hour he must have started in order to begin his return. Robert would arrive back at the base at almost any hour on a Monday morning. Our platoon would fall out for roll call in the darkness of early morning, and if Robert had not returned to answer, I would move to a different position within the platoon, and answer "present" for him. This deception worked well, and eventually he would saunter into our unit without any problems. As I reflect back on those weekends, my answering roll call on his behalf to prevent him from being Absent Without Leave (AWOL) may have been unnecessary as it may have been that he did not have to report back at any prearranged time. If

Robert were the CID agent attached to our company, he would have had either special privileges or a totally different work schedule.

During the time Robert and I were stationed at Camp Pendleton, our headquarters unit was selected to accompany the Dog Company on a field maneuver entitled Operation Ski Lift. Operation Ski Lift was a most unusual name for a field operation as it took place in the Mojave Desert in Nevada. We were to witness an atomic bomb explosion but in truth, we were used as guinea pigs to test the effects of a nuclear blast and subsequent radiation contamination on troops in a combat situation. It wasn't until many years later when researching information for this book that I found that the nuclear guinea pig program in the Mojave Desert was yet another MKULTRA program. It is now part of Area 51 and home to Skunk Works, another division and descendent of the MKULTRA program. As previously explained, Skunk Works is home to the development of fighter planes.

Years later, while on a visit to Robert in California, he told me that I should purchase *American Ground Zero, The Secret Nuclear War* written by Carole Gallagher, as he appeared in the book. It is a collection of photographs and oral histories of those who were affected by radioactive fallout from U.S. nuclear weapons tests performed during the 1950s and 1960s. While reading the book, it came to my attention that in Gallagher's discussion with Robert, she had incorrectly spelled his last name. I questioned Robert as to how Gallagher had selected him from the thousands of young Marines that had been used as nuclear guinea pigs. I also wondered if she had made an honest mistake on his name, was the error purposefully misleading, or if I had misspelled his name for the entire time that I had known him. I also asked him if he had ever tried to obtain his military records and he stated that he had tried once, but was told there were no records found on him. However, he did say there was a sailor with his personal military service number (his records not being found or not existing are completely different situations). This sailor's name just happened to have the same spelling that Gallagher had used in her book. Because of my encounter with the MKULTRA, I now question all discrepancies. I had been fooled twice and will try not to be fooled again.

When I returned from Operation Ski Lift, I was notified that I had been selected to represent Camp Pendleton as a member of the Western Division Rifle Team. This didn't surprise me as I had scored in the top percent of our platoon while in basic training and had qualified for the Expert Rifleman category. Although it was an enviable position that I greatly appreciated, I question why I was given the opportunity to practice and become a member of the team at Camp Matthews in San Diego. In retrospect, I think that this was just another training program that led towards my involuntary programming and indoctrination into the MKULTRA program.

After my return from rifle team training and competition, I was reassigned. Robert and I received orders to leave the 5th Marines and attend teletype school in San Diego. We completed an eight week course and after graduation, returned again to the 5th Marines. However, while Robert remained at that base, I was transferred to main side headquarters in Camp Pendleton. This turned out to be a fortunate transfer for me as base headquarters is where the top performing Marines are positioned.

While I worked at base headquarters, a message came across a teletype machine that requested that a Marine with my MOS of 2511 be required to transfer to Japan to fill an open teletype operator position. I removed the message from the teletype machine and hand-delivered it to the Commanding General's office located just down the hall and requested permission to be the Marine selected to fill the position. The Commanding General questioned me to determine if this is what I really desired and I convinced him that it was. The Naval Air Station in Atsugi (NAS Atsugi) was known as the

Spook Base of the Far East. NAS Atsugi was the Far East's CIA operations center and home of the new MKULTRA, the mind control division of the CIA. I now wonder if my receipt of the message and request for transfer was a mere coincidence as the transfer placed me in the control of the MKULTRA. The saying goes, "nothing by chance" and this is especially true when dealing with the CIA. I have repeatedly tried to recall exactly where I was when the MKULTRA program made its initial contact with me. I believe it was at the Marine Corps Air Station (MCAS) El Toro in Santa Ana, CA, prior to my departure for Japan, but it quite possibly could have been when I was chosen to be a member of the Camp Pendleton Rifle Team while at the 5th Marines.

Our port of departure was in Los Angeles where we were to sail on the USS Anderson. Interestingly, MCAS El Toro was the last base where Oswald was stationed after he returned from Japan. This was prior to his hardship discharge and preceded his being assigned by the MKULTRA to a new mission to the Soviet Union. I arrived in Japan through the harbor in Yokohama in January of 1958. We traveled by bus to NAS Atsugi and arrived in the evening where we were checked in, shown our barracks and designated bunks, and given bedding supplies for the night. I was assigned to become a member of the Marine Air Base Squadron (MABS). Prior to my arrival, the First Marine Air Wing had been deployed on maneuvers to the Philippines and I had not yet met Oswald as he was a member of this deployment. I remained at Atsugi in the Air Wing's absence, and became part of a skeleton crew that operated headquarters as a rear echelon group. Shortly after the return of the Air Wing, I was temporarily transferred to Iwakuni on the island of Honshu, Japan. My transfer stated that I was to attend teletype school to prepare me to be a message center supervisor. I graduated first in my class returned to NAS Atsugi to take on my new duties in the headquarters message center.

One evening shortly after I returned, I was on duty at First Marine Air Wing headquarters message center when I heard the teletype machine give fives spaces - five bells alternating across the carriage of the teletype machine. This code signified a flash message of the highest possible priority. The message read, "Move MAG 11 Formosa." I immediately tore off the message, jumped into the communications Jeep, and speedily hand delivered the message to the officer of the day located on the main side of Atsugi. The First Marine Air Wing was immediately deployed to Formosa, currently known as Taiwan. I recall that I was given special liberty shortly after I received this flash message. When out on liberty in the village of Yamato, I was questioned by the local residents if we were moving our Air Wing to Formosa. The general public's grapevine in the Far East seemed to be equivalent to our top-secret message center for transmitting speedy information. The Air Wing was deployed in support of General Chang Kai-shek's military and its destination was the Nationalist Chinese Air Force base located at Pingtung, Taiwan. Communist Mainland China was bombing the offshore islands of Quemoy and Matsu and also threatened a land invasion to overthrow the Taiwanese government. Now, almost 50 years later, the same saber rattling threat still occurs with the exception that we now have dialog and trade agreements with China. The squadron to which Oswald was attached had located its radar control tracking station in the mountains away from Pingtung. It was the station's responsibility to track all air flights in the area, over the Taiwan Straits, and to track the flights of the top-secret U-2 spy plane. Marine Air Control Squadron One (MACS-1) also handled the radar control for our air strip located in Pingtung. Oswald and another friend of mine, Fred, were stationed with this MACS-1 unit.

Fred

I first met Fred when I was on mess duty, which coincidently, was also the first time I met Oswald. It is certainly possible that Fred was on mess duty to monitor Oswald's behavior or my own. I recall that he was exceptionally well groomed and was referred to as a "squared away" Marine. It is curious that I remember these small details after such a long time. I also remember that I had asked Fred why a Corporal would be given mess duty and he gave me no answer and just cast the question aside. Fred had three unique characteristics that made him stand out among the average Marine. First, he carried the rank of Corporal which did not represent his age or demeanor. Second, Fred always carried pens and pencils in his utility field jacket pocket at all times. Although I realize this is a small detail, it was nonetheless a direct violation of the Marine Corps dress code. When I pointed out this violation, he seemed not the least bit concerned and acted as though regulations did not pertain to him. When we served on mess duty together, he and I became very good friends. But although Oswald and I had a few casual conversations, we never became friends. Fred and I never traveled off base on liberty together; he was what I refer to as a base buddy. However, when Fred was catcher on the Atsugi Flyers baseball team, I accompanied him to the Army base, Camp Zama, to watch a game.

A third detail was the fact that Fred, a non-commissioned officer, wore Cordovan leather shoes. Only Commissioned officers were permitted to wear shoes made of Cordovan as it is a unique and more expensive type of leather. It is made in Cordovan, Italy, from the hide around a horse's ass. I always thought this was the appropriate type of leather to be worn by officers. It is distinctly different in that it has fewer pores and requires less effort to achieve a higher gloss than regular leather. I had asked Fred how he was permitted to wear the Cordovan shoes and he answered convincingly that he had just gone to military supply and purchased them with no questions asked.

Fred was also able to go out on liberty and stay off the base well past midnight. At NAS Atsugi, Marines under the rank of Sergeant were restricted by a Cinderella liberty rule and had to check in at the gate by midnight. If a Marine was over the rank of Sergeant, or had special permission, the Cinderella rule did not apply. I asked Fred how he managed to return to the base night after night and slip by the military police at the gate without creating any problems. His answer seemed very clever to me and at the time, I thought it quite creative. He said he would pass through the Main Gate on the Navy side of Atsugi, flash his identification card, and pretend to be intoxicated when challenged by a gate sentry. He would appear to stagger and then continue in the direction of the officer billeting area which was located next to the main gate. This act, combined with his obvious older appearance, important demeanor, and Cordovan Leather shoes, and also the young gate sentries did not want a confrontation with an apparent officer, this would allow him to pass by unchallenged. I realized that I could never accomplish such a charade as I was a very young looking 19-year old.

I recall one particular day when I served on mess duty that Fred requested I accompany him. He handed me a clipboard and we walked through the mess hall. He pretended to be the "officer of the day" and asked the Marines if they enjoyed their meal and if they had any suggestions as to how the Corps could enhance their dinning experience. I played the part of his assistant and jotted down the answers we received from the interviews. At the time, I thought his actions were brazen; it was a daring prank and impersonating and officer could have severe repercussions. In retrospect, I believe I may have been the only person hoodwinked. In all probability, Fred certainly could have been the "officer of the day" and only carried out the duties that he was required to perform. As I consider Fred's age and demeanor, his Cordovan leather shoes, the pencils in his pocket, his consistent disregard of the Cinderella liberty rule, and his name absent from the MACS-1 roster, I am led to believe that he may have been an intelligence agent and not just a fellow Marine.

I am not certain how Fred enters into the MKULTRA picture, but because he spent such a large amount of time with me, and was in MACS-1 with Oswald, I believe him to be part of the mind control program. There are many discrepancies surrounding Fred including his true identity, his Marine Corps duties, and how he ended up in California after his discharge as Robert's friend (whom he did not know while stationed in Japan). Fred was either an agent for the CIA or another controlled Marine at Atsugi. My inclination leans towards Fred as being an agent of the MKULTRA. He does not appear on the roster of Marines that were attached to MACS-1 during the time Oswald was there although I do have photographic evidence that Fred was indeed attached to MACS-1 at the same point in time. I discovered this discrepancy by accident while I was researching this book. I had not given this much thought until I discovered he did not exist on the MACS-1 squadron roster. Oswald's former commanding officer stated in testimony that he was aware there was a CIA agent operating within the squadron. Was this my friend Fred? If it was, it would explain why his name did not appear on the roster as he was quite possibly not a Marine, but a CIA agent or someone working for the Office of Naval Intelligence as a Marine under cover. It does not surprise me there would be a CIA agent within MACS-1 as they controlled sensitive information that concerned the U-2 spy plane project.

I knew through our friendship that Fred had grown up in Minneapolis, MN. Years later I worked for the Prudential Insurance Company and attended a sales management school in Minneapolis. I decided to contact Fred's family in an attempt to locate him. I made contact with his brother on the telephone and we had a pleasant but short conversation. He informed me that since his discharge, Fred had returned only once to Minnesota to attend his father's funeral. I inquired as to what Fred was doing and where he was living but he said that he did not know what Fred had been involved while he served and never spoke of his Marine Corps days although he informed me that he had remained in California after his discharge.

In Atsugi, MACS-1 was billeted directly across the street from our barracks. As previously mentioned, in Taiwan, MACS-1 was located in the mountains and the remainder of the air wing was located in Pingtung. I saw Fred only once while we were stationed in Pingtung. I recall that I traveled by military Jeep to the MACS-1 mountain location on a very rainy evening. When we arrived, the person who accompanied me ordered me to remain in the vehicle while he made contact with Fred. Unfortunately, this person will always remain faceless to me by what I believe is a controlled memory block. I don't know our reason for being at MACS-1, but Fred came over to the Jeep and said hello to me. To the best of my knowledge, this was the only time I saw or spoke to him while in the Far East. This meeting took place in the spring of 1959 and our unit left Taiwan and arrived back at Yokohama on Easter morning of the same year.

I next spoke to Fred shortly after the Kennedy assassination when Robert phoned me from a party. It was approximately 2 a.m. when I received their call and as a joke, Robert pretended he was a representative of the Federal government. He asked several personal questions that only someone with whom I had an intimate relationship could have known unless they had my personal file in front of them. I was certain that it was a prank, but as it was late and I was only partially awake, I immediately reverted back to my old Marine Corps habits and answered, "yes sir," and "no sir," to the questions. The person asked if I was aware that a war in the Far East, namely Vietnam, was about to break out and I replied, "Yes, sir." It was at that moment I thought the person had made a major mistake when he stated I was familiar with Asian customs and languages as I had not been trained in Asian language or customs. I answered, "No sir." After a few minutes into the conversation I became aware that the person on the phone was Robert and that he was playing a practical joke on me. He broke into laughter and confessed to being at a party and thought it would be fun to call and say hello. He and Fred thought it would be a great gag to jerk me around with the threat that the government contemplated my return to Marine Corps active duty in Vietnam. As you can imagine, I was very troubled by this idea as I was now married and my daughter Tracy was just a year old.

The most unforgettable part of the conversation that night was when Robert told me that Fred was also at the party and wanted to speak to me. Fred got on the phone and my first question to him was, "How do you two know each other?" I knew they had never met when I was stationed with them in either Pingtung or Atsugi. Robert answered that they had met by chance on a San Francisco street and through conversation, found that they both knew me. I have to question the likelihood of this happening as the chance of them accidentally meeting on the street is doubtful. As the Richard Bach saying goes, "nothing by chance." We continued to talk and reminisce but the conversation didn't last long. I find it interesting that the call took place shortly after the Kennedy assassination. In retrospect, I question whether they made contact for old time's sake, or to gauge how much of my past I may have recalled as an MKULTRA mind-controlled Marine. Was this a fact finding call?

As I previously mentioned, I have at minimum, a missing weekend from my memory after I returned to the United States from Japan. I had opted to be stationed at Treasure Island in San Francisco to await an early discharge from the Marines. If I had opted to return to Wisconsin immediately upon my return, I would have had to report to the Great Lakes Naval Training Center in Illinois and receive my discharge there on an original discharge agreement schedule. I believe my missing weekend can be attributed to the government's desire to either teach me a crash course at their Defense Language Institute (DLI) in Monterey or to ascertain whether I was a good candidate to learn a foreign language. It is believed that Oswald was given a crash course in Russian at DLI which would explain his effortless use of the Russian language. It was also believed the DLI had developed a technique that was used to teach a foreign language rapidly and subliminally through the use of drugs or hypnosis. It is entirely possible that I participated in an Asian language program of which Robert may have had knowledge.

More than 20 years later I traveled to California to speak with Robert and discovered he had phoned Fred, who called me at my daughter Jill's hotel room in Salinas. Fred decided to accompany me on the trip to Big Sur where Robert lived. During our drive, the name of Steve Short entered the conversation, and I was completely surprised that both Robert and Fred knew him. Steve was another Atsugi Marine and has always been a real mystery to me. To the best of my knowledge, I met Steve only once during our deployment to Taiwan. Robert and I went on liberty together in Pingtung, and Steve, whom I had never met nor seen on the base, decided to join us. Robert seemed to know him well. Steve carried the rank of Sergeant but I don't know to which unit he was attached, but I think it was either MACS-1 or possibly the CIA. I never saw Steve again after that evening in Pingtung and would never have remembered him if it were not for an unusual incident that took place that evening.

I had contracted a Taiwanese craftsman to carve a statue of an Old Age Buddha out of camphor wood. I had already paid for the order and was having difficulty getting the craftsman to complete the statue. As I was trying to talk to the craftsman, Steve asked me what the problem was. After I told him, he walked into the man's shop and shouted at him in a thunderous voice. Initially, I though he was pretending to speak Chinese but the craftsman responded to his every word. I had thought by the craftsman's demeanor and the other Taiwanese present that he was merely responding to Steve's attitude, but then realized that Steve was indeed speaking Chinese. This really surprised me and I asked him where he had learned the language but he ignored my question. At that point in time, it was quite astonishing for a Marine Corps Sergeant to speak fluent Chinese.

It wasn't until years later, when Robert phoned to tell me he was flying into Madison, WI, that I thought of Steve. Robert had contacted me and wondered if I could meet him somewhere. My home in Viroqua, WI, was just a couple of hours away from Madison. He reminded me that he had made a promise that if he ever traveled in my direction, he would stop by to visit. He was working as a salesman for National Screw and Manufacturing located in San Francisco and was passing through the area on his way to Salt Lake City, UT. As I didn't know Madison that well and couldn't think of a good meeting place, Robert suggested that we meet at the Statler Hotel across from the Greyhound Bus station. At the time, I did not question his knowledge of the Statler Hotel even though it was his first trip to Madison. When I met him I recalled that he looked very different from my memory of him. This was the third time that I noticed an evident change in his appearance. The first time was in Kaohsiung, Taiwan, when I noticed his wavy hair and lack of a dead tooth. The second time he appeared different to me was in the mountains of Taiwan. As I walked down the mountainside and into a small village, he ran out of a small building and it was his body language and gait that still lingered in my memory as he was very tall and lanky. As I now watched him stride across the hotel lobby, I thought that his posture and gait again seemed different.

During our rendezvous, Robert told me he had traveled to Vietnam during the war after his discharge from the Marines. This surprised me as he had always told me that his goal was to live the life of a commercial fisherman on a boat docked at Fisherman's Wharf in Monterey. His service in Vietnam was a striking deviation from his life goal. Because of this, I asked him why he had chosen to serve and he explained that he had met Steve Short and became involved with his sister and that Steve had offered him a job at his import business. I asked him what his duties were as an importer in a Vietnam War zone. He gave me the vague answer that he flew around in a helicopter and catalogued the head count of the troops. I remarked that the military would already have this information and what he had tried to accomplish just did not make sense. It was then that he looked at me and told me that he just did not understand what he was doing. Robert did not know, or he did not know how to explain, what he had been doing, and gave me a puzzled gaze as though this was the first time he had thought about why he was in Vietnam. He also revealed that he had become victim of some type of bacteria while he was there and that a portion of his large intestine had been removed and that he now wore a colostomy bag. Later, when I visited Robert at his home in California, I asked him how he was doing with regards to this health problem and the colostomy bag and he informed me that he had the process reversed. I also inquired about his dead tooth and he replied that he had the gold removed and earrings made out of it for his daughter. When I recalled Robert's appearance prior to this meeting, I remembered that he never had any gold in his tooth and that it was a discolored gray hue because it was dead. This Robert, Robert-2, always seemed to have an answer for every question I presented. But why would I question that he was not my good friend and that a double, placed there by the government, may have pretended to be Robert.

My wife accompanied me to Madison the day I went to visit Robert, who I believe was really Robert-2. On the ride home, I asked her what she remembered most about the afternoon. She said she was amazed that Robert and I spoke only about politics as she expected us to do a fair amount of reminiscing. She stated that she never knew I was so interested in politics, and at that time, I hadn't been. I experienced a strange feeling on the way home and I believe it was due to what my wife had pointed out; the fact that Robert and I had not reminisced about our time together in the Marine Corps. Robert-2 had brought a lady friend along for the afternoon. He said that she was an old girlfriend who worked in the psychology department at the University of Wisconsin. I wonder now if she really was an old girlfriend, or someone working for government intelligence.

The connection between Robert-2, Fred, and Steve seems strange when you consider they were all Atsugi Marines. Supposedly, they did not know each other while at Atsugi but ended up together in San Francisco. While he worked for Steve, Robert-2 made a major detour in his life when he traveled to the jungles of Vietnam during the height of the war. In my research I have found no record of the National Screw and Manufacturing Company and I believe that the company that Robert-2 and Steve worked for in San Francisco may have been a "dummy corporation" and possibly a front for the real company, the CIA. I often wonder about the night Robert and Fred telephoned me in Wisconsin and if their practical joke was actually a recruiting ploy to have me join them on whatever Vietnam mission they were about to enter into with Steve.

It is when I was stationed in Pingtung that I first recall some bizarre incidents taking place. For more than six months I had watched the overseas draft arrive from the United States in hopes of seeing a familiar face. After a period of time, I gave up the watch and realized that any Marine I might have known back in the US would be on a short-timers list. As they would have a limited amount of time left in the Corps, they would not be transferred for overseas duty. The rule of thumb was that one should have at least 18 months of military service remaining in order to make it beneficial for the government to transfer a Marine to a foreign duty station. As I rode in the back of a military truck one afternoon in Pingtung, we passed a group of Marines that had just arrived as replacements. From out of the new group a familiar voice yelled, "Hey Hawk!" It was my friend Robert from the 5th Marines. I was pleased to see him and asked how he had been selected to be in the Far East with so little time left to serve. He replied that he didn't know how his assignment had come about, which may or may not be true, and I didn't question him any further. Robert was placed on my shift in the message center where I was supervisor. He also became the newest member of our group's tent, which consisted of only four Marines, and was issued the bunk next to mine. The odds of Robert being transferred into a combat zone in the Far East as a short-timer, working in headquarters on my shift, and sleeping in the bunk next time mine, were astonishing.

Because we served in a combat zone, our shifts at the message center were very long. We worked 12 hours on- and 12 hours off-duty and had little time for anything else. When we could get away, we often would walk through a banana grove to a river and would idle away the afternoon by swimming and relaxing among the farmers working in their fields. Unfortunately, the river eventually became off limits. When we did receive liberty, Robert and I would go into Pingtung at every opportunity. On our first trip together into the city, located a couple of miles outside the main gate, we met two Chinese officers who became our good friends. I recall they had followed us at a distance around Pingtung for most of the afternoon before they tried to make contact with us. Both spoke excellent English and I thought this was unusual at the time. I asked them how they knew English but didn't have any reason to think that anything subversive was taking place. In the 1950s it would have been extremely unlikely that Chinese military personnel would have been afforded the opportunity to study and speak English. They would only have been able to speak English if they served in some capacity as part of Chinese military intelligence. I was only 19 years old at the time and extremely naïve. I looked upon the Chinese military officers as only assisting us in finding our way around Pingtung. Why should I suspect that my new friend, Yeh Wah Chu, and his buddy could have been intelligence operatives for the Chinese military? In retrospect, it seems fairly obvious that they were and I wonder if it was the Chinese Military or the CIA, or both, that used and controlled Oswald, Robert, and me.

Yeh Wah Chu, far right.

Over the succeeding months, Robert and I frequently visited Yeh Wah Chu and his friends at their barracks on the Chinese side of the base. We would make multiple excursions into Pingtung together and on one trip, we were introduced to a rather large woman from the Philippines who told us she spoke seven languages. She asked Robert and me if we would help with a girl's school in Pingtung. We were asked if we would consider teaching young businesswomen how to speak sufficient English to assist them as they conducted business with visiting Marines. At the time, I never questioned the fact that both she and Yeh Wah Chu spoke very good English. I also didn't consider that I might be used by these people, as I worked within the Marine Corps headquarter message center and handled top-secret information. I never gave a second thought about the very sensitive material I handled every day, or that Yeh Wah Chu and his friends might be Communist Chinese and not necessarily loyal to the Nationalist Chinese cause. I have no idea if Robert was aware of what was occurring and he may have been just as duped as I was. However, I now know that one of the Roberts was aware of what was taking place and that most likely it was Robert-2. I often wonder if he worked for either the Nationalist or Communist Chinese, or the CIA.

The first time I became aware that I had met Robert's double was in Kaohsiung, Taiwan. We were to meet in the city square but unfortunately, I don't remember the purpose of our meeting. This isn't that strange as I traveled to many unknown places in the Far East without apparent reason; I would just arrive at a destination and not understand how I got there or why I was there. Kaohsiung is a considerable distance from Pingtung and no buses or other modes of public transportation were available so it was a most unusual spot for us to meet. That particular evening was very strange. Robert-2 did not arrive when expected, so I waited near our rendezvous point in an upstairs bar in the middle of a market square. While I waited for him to arrive, an American businessman approached my table and introduced himself. I had noticed that the man had been observing me and was most likely instructed to keep me entertained until Robert-2 arrived. Kaohsiung is a very remote city and it was highly unusual to meet an American in this location, especially in a small out-of-the-way bar in a war zone. I don't recall the details of our conversation but the man told me that he was the Vice President of Kaiser Motor Company in the United States.

I waited a few hours past our scheduled meeting time and Robert-2 finally arrived. The first thing I noticed about him was his perfect white teeth. During the time I had known him, he had always had a dead front tooth that was discolored and considerably darker than the surrounding teeth. I also noticed that his hair was very wavy, where it had previously been straight. I asked him about these changes in his appearance and although he didn't comment about his tooth, he explained that he had a permanent at a hair salon earlier in the day which may have accounted for his extreme tardiness. Permanents were not something that Marines did to their hair in 1958, but at the time, I was satisfied with his answer. At that point, I had no reason to believe anything else, such as this man was not the 'real' Robert. I often wonder where the CIA or other outfit kept Robert while I was with Robert-2. Was Robert involved, or was he abducted and kept somewhere while they performed whatever their mission was to be. Perhaps the plan was merely to introduce Robert-2 to see how I would handle the situation. Would I recognize him as a double? And, if so, how would I react?

I am absolutely certain this encounter was the first time I met Robert-2 and question why the MKULTRA would place an imposter before me. He was accompanied by two Chinese women that he said were nurses and told me that one was his girlfriend; however, I knew he did not have a girlfriend the day before. The fact that they were nurses did not alarm me at the time. The four of us walked a distance and then entered a building that was comprised of just one long narrow room. The only piece of furniture that I saw was a bed at the far end of the room. One of the women told me to lie down on the bed, which I did. That is the last memory that I recall until the following morning when I found myself out on the street, but not next to the building I had entered the night before. As I tried to orient myself, I watched many men parade by dressed in Chinese dragon costumes. They were celebrating the Chinese New Year and I remember fireworks exploding everywhere. Unfortunately, this is my only recollection of that time until I am magically transported back to the base in Pingtung.

When I look back, I am surprised at how easily I was deceived. On the other hand, the year was 1958 and I was just 19 years old and quite naïve. It is obvious that I was controlled by drugs, hypnosis, or a combination of the two. I had traveled to Kaohsiung to meet my friend Robert and even though I noticed several discrepancies in his appearance, I had no reason to think that he could be anyone but my friend. I could not have been aware or even imagined that the MKULTRA used me for some type of clandestine activity. At that time, I didn't know the program existed and certainly could not have been more unsuspecting. Now, I am very angry that I was taken advantage of without my knowledge or consent. Who gave them the right to control another individual? Oswald, Robert, and I joined the United States Marine Corps to honorably serve our country. Who gave these Spooks the right to violate us?

My meeting with Robert in Kaohsiung was just one of my many unusual experiences while serving in Japan. On another occasion, our friend, the Chinese officer Yeh Wah Chu, asked Robert and me if we would like to go on a weekend excursion into the mountains to visit an aboriginal village. Robert and I eagerly accepted the invitation and Yeh Wah Chu made the travel arrangements. I don't recall our departure from the base in Pingtung, but only remember our arrival by bus in the mountains after a considerable train ride. It is difficult to describe the entire day as I have only fragmented memories, but do have a vague recollection of traveling past rice paddies while on the train. Years later, when I visited Robert in California, I asked him what he could recall about that day. He said he remembered almost nothing, and that fact had always puzzled him. He remembered the train ride through the countryside and being at the foot of the mountains. I told him about our mountain climb to the aboriginal village with Chinese military personnel, but he stated that he never made the hike. It was in this village that I had taken a photo of Robert-2 and when I showed Robert the image, his wife exclaimed, "that's not Robert!" Robert's expression when he saw the photo was one of sincere surprise. I was careful not to prompt his wife's answer in any way as I wanted an honest and unsolicited answer to confirm what I had already known; the man in the photograph was not Robert, but his double. Robert told me that he had no idea what he had done that afternoon and I suspect he was stored or "put on ice". Therefore, I now knew that I had made the mountain climb with the Chinese officers and military personnel with Robert-2; Robert's doppelganger. I had traveled 2,500 miles from Wisconsin to the cliffs overlooking the Pacific in California for that single affirmation.

It was when I was in the mountain village with Robert-2 that Oswald appeared on the scene. I had previously met him while on mess duty at Atsugi where we had several conversations so I quickly recognized him. I don't know how he arrived in the village or why he was there but I recall that he was very nervous and appeared to be frightened. He paced back and forth in a small building we had entered with the Chinese military personnel. During this time, I did not speak to him as he paced in front of me. I noticed that he had torn the seat of his pants and his butt was covered with dirt. Just prior to his arrival, I had heard someone scream, which sounded like a very painful scream, from the mountain's foothills, and this concerned me. I walked to the edge of the trail and peered over the rim of the hill where I saw a man being handcuffed. I took a photograph of this incident which I still have in my possession. When I leaned over the hill to gather a glimpse of what was happening, the imposter, Robert-2, told me that what was taking place was none of my concern and ordered me to rejoin them on the trail. I obeyed his order but was perplexed as to why I followed his command. Was Robert-2 my controller? I have read in

Oswald's Marine service record that he had been sent back to Atsugi for disciplinary reasons shortly after his arrival in Taiwan. The disciplinary reasons had to do with his discharge of a pistol in his barracks shortly before the Air Wing departed for Taiwan. If this is true, then how did he travel back to the mountain village in Taiwan and why? Obviously, Oswald had received help and permission, and was controlled.

Man being handcuffed, lower left near bridge.

Some time during the afternoon, Robert-2 disappeared unnoticed by me and this must have taken place while we were in the aboriginal village. When I came down the mountainside and entered another small village, Robert-2 ran out of a small thatched roof building and shouted, "Let's get the hell out of here!" He seemed very frightened and consequently, I became very aware of my surroundings and ran with him from the village. During our getaway, we came to a bridge above a very turbulent river. Numerous wooden planks had been removed that made the bridge inaccessible and served as a barrier to keep unwanted people and vehicles out of the village while we were there with the Chinese

Military. There were no other Americans on the mountain that day besides Robert-2, Oswald and I. I have no idea where they kept my friend, the original Robert. When I asked Robert where he thought he had been he said he had no recollection of the entire afternoon. At the time, I had never questioned what had taken place that day. Only later when I reviewed my photographs after Robert told me he never climbed the mountain, did I realize that something was amiss. Robert had not questioned his missing day until I presented him the photograph of his double. He had such an amazed look on his face when I explained what had taken place and described the use of a doppelganger. I believe that Robert had always thought he was a part of something special, but at that moment, just like Oswald, he realized he had been a "patsy."

Bridge to aboriginal village; Oswald is behind first military officer and Robert-2 is behind two other officers with arms outstretched.

Unfortunately, I don't remember what happened after Robert-2 and I had escaped from the aboriginal village. My next memory is that of us walking down a grassy hill and

116

approaching a large beautiful lake. I remember thousands of lily pads in the crystal clear water and two beautiful pagodas with large rusted iron dragon statues guarding them. As I approached the pagodas I saw that Robert-2 had already arrived and was speaking with many Chinese military personnel. Although I did not notice Oswald after we left the mountain village, he may have been in the pagoda with Robert-2. I attempted to walk up the ramp that led to the Pagoda where I had seen Robert-2, but was blocked by Yeh Wah Chu who told me I could not enter. Yeh Wah Chu remained with me and made certain that I did not attempt to enter the Pagoda. Clearly I was under some type of control and did not insist upon entrance. Instead, I remained outside and took several photographs. How I arrived back at the base from the Pagoda is a mystery to me. Robert and I were magically transported back to the base in Pingtung and neither of us questioned nor wondered what transpired that day. I'm not sure we could have traveled with the Chinese officers without the Marine Corps and the CIA being aware as we had top-secret clearance and worked in the headquarter message center. And, they would have also known that Oswald worked in the MACS-1 control tower where he tracked the flights of the top-secret U-2 spy plane.

During my excursion into the mountains, I took many photographs and later showed them to Robert-2 when back at the base in Pingtung. He asked if he could have some of the photos and offered to exchange them with some of the photos that he had taken that day. I was reluctant to hand them over, but remembered I could make more copies from the negatives. He gave me only a few of his photos in return for those of mine he had taken. And, much to my chagrin, my negatives mysteriously disappeared; probably due to a midnight requisition by Robert-2. Of course I had not considered that anything unusual had taken place in the mountain village and had no reason to suspect that he would remove any incriminating photos and negatives. However, one of the photos he gave me in exchange was perhaps one of the most incriminating. It was a photo that someone had taken of him standing on the mountainside. It was the same photo that Robert's wife had seen and declared was not him.

A few days after we returned to the base in Pingtung, a directive was posted that informed Robert and I that we were no longer worthy of proficiency pay. This was highly unusual as I had passed all proficiency pay tests, had qualified for meritorious Corporal rank, and had graduated first in my class at teletype school in Iwakuni. Additionally, I had already received proficiency pay for several months and when I reexamined my military records, I discovered that I had received excellent job performance grades during this time. I was also removed from my supervisory position in the message headquarters section by Captain Cline. He told me that I had become a negative influence upon the troops and that the younger Marines had begun to emulate me. I was only 20 years old at the time and apparently portrayed a negative image of what a Marine should represent. I was disciplined with a transfer to a Guard Company where I became a member of the military police (MP) and assumed the position of Corporal of the Guard. I was very upset with this transfer and complained to Captain Cline. He told me to look at the transfer not as a failure, but to accept it as an opportunity. I told him that I disagreed and didn't view it as an opportunity. I was even more infuriated to learn that Robert remained on duty in the message center. I later realized that the reason I was removed from the message center was to prevent me from recognizing Robert-2 as an imposter. The Marine Corps would have had to be complicit along with the MKULTRA or the Office of Naval Intelligence (ONI) to have been able to move me from one section to another. I wonder whether or not the Marines or ONI knew what really occurred, or if they were also duped by the MKULTRA. Captain Cline was the officer in command of message center headquarters and was obviously aware of what had occurred and assisted in my removal from the facility. However, he would not have noticed the difference between the two Roberts as he did not know either of them well. Was Captain Cline also being duped?

I later discovered that Robert had also been removed from the message center and spent the remainder of his time working on the docks in the Kaohsiung harbor. This conclusively proves that Robert-2 was moved into the message center headquarters after Robert and I had been removed. I had few conversations with Robert-2 during the time I was an MP. I thought my friend Robert had remained in the message center and was perplexed by his indifferent attitude. His actions puzzled me and his avoidance of me was completely out of character. I now realize that he avoided me so that I would not discover his true identity. I am still nagged by the question of who controlled Robert and me and why we needed to be removed from the message center if we had traveled with only the Chinese military into the mountains. Was it the Marine Corps, Naval Intelligence, or the CIA who made this decision? Had either the Communist or Nationalist Chinese infiltrated our headquarters message center? Had multiple factions of the intelligence community infiltrated it?

One afternoon as Robert-2 left the message center I noticed he carried a large volume of papers. When I asked him where he was going, he replied that he was on his way to Pingtung to teach an English class to the young Taiwanese business women that we were supposed to teach together. I was very disappointed at being excluded from the opportunity because of my transfer from the message center. When I asked him about the many papers he carried he explained that they were copies of teaching materials. I reminded him that he could get into serious trouble if it was found out that he had removed papers from the headquarters message center but this did not seem to bother him. Of course, and unbeknownst to me, the Robert I knew was on the docks of Kaohsiung harbor and Robert-2 had now been successfully positioned in the message center.

A few situations that took place while I was in Taiwan have continued to puzzle me. On one of my visits to see Robert he talked about the awful things that the Marine Corps had made us do. I asked him to explain as I couldn't remember anything that we were forced to do that was so terrible. Tears came to his eyes and he spoke about a day that we had gone swimming in a river that flowed near our base in Pingtung. The river was a short walk from our tent area and although it was eventually off-limits, we spent many afternoons there. Robert spoke about a particular afternoon when we had witnessed a young boy that was shot and killed by Chinese soldiers. He said that we had been ordered to not report the incident but that I had become furious, disobeyed the order, and reported the murder. I was shocked to hear Robert tell this story as I did not remember the incident. However, as he related the story, I became very uneasy and agitated, got chills, and noticed that the hair stood up on my arms. I believe this physical response was my subconscious over-riding my programmed memory loss. I know I am controlled by the MKULTRA and continue to try and break though the mental barriers, but with no avail. Obviously the murder of the young boy had been removed from my memory. This feat was accomplished either through hypnosis, drugs, subliminal suggestion, or possibly a combination of techniques. Whenever I think of that day, I feel as though I can almost recall the shooting, but it appears as a vague dream and just out of reach.

On the other hand, I do have a very vivid memory of a day when Robert and I discussed hypnotism with some of the Marines who bunked in our tent. Robert stated that he could hypnotize almost anyone, so I challenged him to hypnotize me. I was adamant that he could not do it and I recall him dangling his dog tags in front of me, improvising on the classic swinging watch method. When his demonstration was complete I said, "See I told you that you could not hypnotize me." Everyone in the tent gave me an unusual look and I discovered that I had, indeed, been hypnotized and was the only one in the tent not aware of this fact.

Our position of duty in Taiwan was classified as a combat zone and therefore we were given Rest and Recuperation (R&R) leave. At that time a Marine had to certify that he had a minimum of one hundred dollars in cash before he would be flown to Hong Kong at the government's expense. I recall that I lent Robert enough money for him to take advantage of the R&R benefit but we did not make the journey together as he had traveled on an earlier schedule. My R&R to Hong Kong was during the 1958 Christmas season. As Hong Kong was then a British Crown Colony, I was able to hear Christmas Carols played via outdoor speakers in the shopping district. Even though I had never been to the city, I found my way around as though I was very familiar with my surroundings. At some point, I became aware that a Chinese man followed me but at the time I cast it off as someone just looking for a homosexual encounter. Although I remember the Chinese man, I am also aware that I was followed by other individuals but they remain faceless. I know I was trailed in the Tiger Balm Garden, on a Peak Tram ride, and at an evening meal aboard the Sea Palace, a large floating restaurant in the Hong Kong harbor. This evening meal remains especially clear in my memory. I stayed at the Princess Hotel on the Kowloon side of the bay and rode the Starr Ferry across the bay to Hong Kong. I met some people whom I did not know and also remain faceless to me. We traveled by sampan, a flat-bottomed Chinese wooden boat, and sailed among the Chinese Junks out to the Sea Palace. As we entered the restaurant I noticed that the door was just above the water level and we passed a large aquarium containing numerous different types of fish - - our menu. I selected a large red fish for my meal and we then climbed a flight of stairs to our dining area. I sat at a table with several people but don't recall any conversation and when I try to remember them, they seem like ghosts. As I look back upon that evening meal, I am convinced that I was being con-trolled and have had my memory altered to erase faces and conversations.

Because it was Christmas, I purchased gifts and cards for my family and stopped at the Hong Kong Post Office to have them delivered with a Hong Kong postmark. All my mail from the Far East was usually sent home via the Fleet Post Office in San Francisco. I thought my family back in Wisconsin would really enjoy the novelty of receiving mail directly from Hong Kong. However, when I asked my family if they enjoyed the stamps and postmarks they told me they had never received any mail with Hong Kong postage. I believe my mail had been opened and examined and then resent through the customary Fleet Post Office. Perhaps the Chinese man who trailed me was a MKULTRA agent and knew that I had sent mail.

I spent three days in Hong Kong on my leave and was accompanied the entire time by someone who guided me, yet remains invisible. To this day only a few memories remain of that time. I can recall being accompanied one morning by a large and very well dressed Caucasian man, approximately 50 years old and who I believe was European. His wife and beautiful red-haired daughter accompanied us. I desired to purchase a tailor-made suit and the gentleman guided me to

Mohan's, an exceptional clothing shop. Interestingly, when I described this experience to Robert, he said he had been to the very same store for his tailored clothing. I think this is an extraordinary coincidence in a long line of coincidences.

I have also been plagued by several other vaporous memories of my R&R leave. I recall being in a dark and dingy smoke filled opium den where I observed many elderly Chinese men lying around on the floor and in stacked beds. And, on what I think was the same evening, I played the game *GO* in an upstairs apartment with several women. I know I also passed by a leper colony each morning on my way to a destination that remains unknown. I also remember that at some point I was very frightened and ran down the hillside streets to escape from someone. This last memory is the clearest and I frequently dream of this, and always in color. During all of these events, I was accompanied by those faceless individuals. I also have no recollection of my trip back to the airport or my flight back to Pingtung. It is obvious to me that during this trip, the MKULTRA was in control of me. Although these memories are faint and murky, I remember the rest of my Hong Kong trip with great clarity.

Next to the US Air Force, Air America is the second largest air force in the world and is operated by the CIA out of Taipei, Taiwan. Our Air Wing spent approximately nine months in Taiwan and returned to Atsugi on Easter Sunday in 1959 via an LST loaded with trucks and communication equipment. It is after my return to Atsugi when things became surreal.

After my removal from the message center I became a member of the Guard Company. I performed sentry duty at the main gate at the base and checked both vehicles and Marines on and off the base. After my transfer, it seemed as though no one was concerned about what happened to me. It was shortly after I was placed as a sentry that I believe the MKULTRA used me again as a controlled Marine and, unfortunately, I recall very little during this time as I was a victim of mind control. I became a road patrol MP and patrolled the road between Kaishiung and Pingtung with the sergeant of the guard.

As Corporal of The Guard, my work shifts alternated and it would have been impossible for me to have traveled around Japan and Taiwan without the military or MKULTRA being complicit in my role as a Manchurian Candidate. I have very fragmented memories of this time and would often find myself outside the base at the MKULTRA Bluebird bar or on a train in Tokyo. At times I would gain sudden clarity and not know where I was or what I was doing, and then slip back into a kind of dream state. I traveled by train from Yamotomachi to Yokohama almost every weekend. Upon arrival in Yokohama, I would immediately go to a German restaurant for lunch. I don't remember a desire to go there, just that I had a pressing need to be there. I had the same meal (meatballs, carrots, potatoes, and gravy) each time and everyone in the restaurant attentively watched me eat. Aside from eating lunch, I have no idea what I did in the city or where I went. I can only conclude that I must have been some type of courier and the restaurant was my control location. However, as I was no longer attached to the message center, I would not have had access to top-secret information unless Robert-2 gave it to me without my knowledge. For this reason, I believe that I was a study in progress and was scrutinized to see how I would perform.

I returned to Atsugi still attached to the Guard Company and it was there that I was given sentry duty and assigned to walk the post that encircled the top-secret U-2 spy plane hangar. One Sunday morning a scheduled sentry was ill and I acted as a supernumerary to replace him out of necessity. Requiring a Corporal of the Guard to work a different schedule was highly unusual as a sentry post is usually designated to be patrolled by a Private or Private First Class Marine, not the Corporal of the Guard. I was driven to my post by the Sergeant of The Guard and issued a 12-gauge

Remington pump shotgun. As I began my rounds, I was overcome with extreme fatigue and drowsiness and had great difficulty keeping my eyes open. I walked to a geodesic dome that was used as a storage building for Sidewinder Missiles and curled up on the rough gravel floor to sleep. I remained asleep for my entire four hour shift and only awakened by the sound of a guard truck engine that had arrived with a new sentry to relieve me from my post. Had anyone discovered me I would have suffered serious consequences and been given an automatic court-martial, time in the brig, loss of rank and pay grade, and a colossal blemish on my excellent military record. I would have violated one of the major General Orders to, "walk my post in a military manner keeping always on the alert, and observing everything that takes place within sight or hearing." My slumber was a serious infraction of military code, especially when it took place while I was to have guarded the most highly guarded secret the US Government had at the time, the U-2 spy plane. Not to mention that the infraction took place in a foreign country at the height of the Cold War. I understood the severe consequences of my actions but it was impossible for me to remain awake. Was I programmed to get caught, but escaped penalty when I overheard the guard truck approaching? Was I placed in this compromising situation to allow something illegal or clandestine to take place? Or, was this simply part of my mind control training to see how much power they had over me?

One evening I was in a small marketplace in Yokohama with Robert-2 and an American civilian. Robert-2 had purchased what he said was Benzedrine (amphetamine) and asked me to try some. I complied and recall that the drug made me very alert and talkative. I am not aware if drugs were a problem in the military at that time but doubt if there was a penalty for Benzedrine use. While on the drug, the American civilian made a very unusual statement. He told me that if I ever had any problems to contact an address that he then instructed me to write down. I questioned him why I should have any problems and if I did, how he could possibly help me. Although he did not answer my questions, I copied the address he gave me on the back of my 1956 Wisconsin driver's license. As I was under the influence of Benzedrine, the address did not make any sense to me when I glanced at it later. After my license expired, I tossed it into a box of memorabilia and did not give it a second thought.

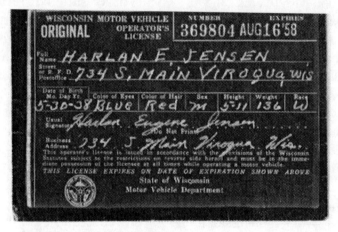

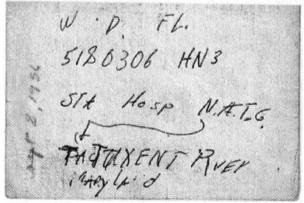

Hawk's 1958 Driver's License Copy, Front and Back

Years later, as I watched the movie *The Hunt for Red October*, I noticed a digital message that scrolled across the bottom of the screen during a scene in which a submarine progressed down a river. The scrolling message referred to the Patuxent River in Maryland. I became very anxious and when I arrived home from the movie theatre I immediately searched through my box of military memorabilia. I pulled out my 1956 driver's license and discovered the address I had written on the back so many years before was that of the Naval Health Clinic headquartered in Patuxent River, MD. Once I had finally discovered the location of the address on my license, I began to contemplate why the American civilian I had met more than 30 years ago was so concerned about my welfare. Apparently, he was concerned enough to give me contact information for the naval hospital with instructions to get in touch with someone there if I needed help in any way. In the 1950s, the trip to Patuxent River would have been an arduous journey that would have taken weeks to complete. I know now that the naval hospital had connections with the CIA and can only surmise that the MKULTRA had intended to stay in contact with me past my military service. Moreover, I find it troubling that it was anticipated that I would experience future medical problems.

I believe I was also under the influence of drugs one night while I was in the Guard Company Quonset hut. However, I could have been almost anyplace as I don't remember ever sleeping in those barracks even though it was the unit to which I was attached. As I lay on my bunk I could feel my heart race and pound as thought it were going to explode in my chest. Although I was somewhat delirious, I remember that fellow Marines would stop by my bunk and talk about what might be wrong with me, and I heard others instruct them to leave me alone. By that time I may have been under full control of the MKULTRA. Something prompted me to try and escape from the situation and I recall that I cried, and that was something I just did not do. Somehow I knew the only safe haven for me would be the church and that I needed to gain assistance from the Chaplin. As I attempted to escape the area, a Marine ordered me to halt or he would shoot. I just continued to walk and at any moment expected to hear the crack of a rifle. I can't imagine why such extreme measures would have been taken to prevent me from leaving the area as I had done nothing wrong and only wanted to speak to the Chaplain. Despite the threat of being shot, I arrived safely at the Chapel and spoke with Chaplin Dodge. I explained my situation to him as best as I could but I didn't fully understand the situation myself. I don't know how Chaplin Dodge handled the situation, but what had happened to me in regards to my state of disorientation and control by the MKULTRA ceased for the few months that I had left of my overseas service. However, I think it is possible that they continued to use me in their program, but just kept me in limbo for that time for I know that their program began again once I arrived in San Francisco.

The first evening that we were home we were shuttled off to Treasure Island, a Naval Base that was located in the San Francisco Bay. It was the same evening that an infamous escape from Alcatraz took place, and the next morning I strolled down to the beach near the barracks and scanned the rocky beach as I thought the convict may have drowned and his body washed ashore.

As previously mentioned, when a Marine arrives at Treasure Island, he is given the option to travel home immediately on leave. After leave had been completed, he would report to the nearest duty station for permanent discharge on a preset schedule. Or, he would be reassigned dependent on how much time he had left to serve under his initial enlistment agreement. A second option would be to remain at Treasure Island Naval Station and, for the convenience of the government, receive an early discharge. I opted to stay and receive an early discharge which would give me an opportunity to visit San Francisco. While at Treasure Island my days were occupied by someone who once again controlled my daily movements. Robert and I spent a lot of time in San Francisco but I have no idea what we did there as my memory is shadowy from that time period. I do recall visiting the Purple Onion, a popular nightclub. Mort Sahl,

the popular comedian and political activist was being featured the evening we were there. Robert said he knew Mort and after the show told me to remain out in front of the club while he went backstage to speak to him. He never explained how he knew Sahl or why he had to speak to him. We also frequented a night club called the Jazz Workshop where the Kingston Trio performed. One afternoon when we were in an Italian section of the city, we entered a small wine, bread, and sausage shop. Robert traced his hand on a piece of paper and colored it in and then instructed me to give it to the man and woman by the cash register in the front of the shop. I handed them the paper and they shouted obscenities at me. Robert ran from the shop and I followed at his heels. Robert revealed that the colored hand was a Mafia death sign that indicated that they were going to be eliminated. I have no idea why Robert did this unless he thought it to be a practical joke. The shopkeepers certainly found no humor in the situation. I believe that this could possibly have been another test or element of control training that was being performed on me.

During this period we also had a conversation with a very strange looking individual outside a movie theatre in downtown San Francisco. I thought it was very unusual that Robert told me not to have anything to do with the man. I can't imagine that I would have had anything to do with him even if Robert had not instructed me otherwise. I can't be certain, but from photos and various renderings I believe the man was David Ferrie. Ferrie was a prime suspect in the Kennedy assassination investigation and kept reappearing in Oswald's life. He maintained that he had hypnotized Oswald and was his controller.

I was not aware at the time that the MKULTRA was operating safe houses through the CIA in San Francisco. The safe houses' primary purpose was to entice unsuspecting young men to enter for sexual favors either with prostitutes or homosexuals. Agents would remain hidden behind walls and mirrors to watch and film the unsuspecting individuals

They would gather information for study and sometimes for blackmail. Unfortunately, a friend and I spent an evening at one of those houses after being solicited on the street. It wasn't until years later that I realized we had been involved in yet another clandestine MKULTRA program.

One day while back at the Treasure Island base, Robert asked me if I would like to accompany him to his home town of Monterey for the weekend. I had read all of John Steinbeck's books which depicted the wine country around Monterey and especially wanted to see Cannery Row. We boarded a Greyhound bus in San Francisco and Robert had brought along a flask full of wine which surprised me as drinking had never been part of our friendship. It also surprised me that he shared the wine with the bus driver who proceeded to drink and drive. I believe I was given drugs either via the wine or from a sandwich as the last clear memory I can recall of that weekend was the Greyhound bus pulling up to the bus stop outside the Fort Ord Army base.

Obviously I was drugged and under some type of control and Robert was definitely my controller. I faintly remember driving by Cannery Row and Robert informing me of this fact, although I don't know how we had obtained a car. I was lying in the back seat and I struggled to rise and peer out the window. However, I could not bring myself up to the window and it was as though I was being held down by invisible hands. My next memory is of being on a beach at night and I was still lying in the backseat of the car. Robert was drinking and conversing with people next to a large open fire and I wanted to join them but again was unable to haul myself out of the car. I remained in the car overnight and had no idea where we had stayed. Robert told me he wanted to visit his ex-wife who lived in a small home on the beach. The invisible force still held me in the car and I watched him speak to a woman at the front door of a bungalow. During the weekend I also remember that we visited a small café in Carmel and he instructed me to remain in the cafe until his return. I have no idea why I obeyed his

command and after he had been gone a considerable time, I became anxious but could not bring myself to leave the cafe to find him. Amazingly, I can't remember the trip back to San Francisco and seem to have been mysteriously transported back to the base on Treasure Island.

It has been revealed Oswald had possibly attended the Defense Language Institute Foreign Language Center in Monterey. This would have been about the same time I experienced my missing weekend in Monterey. Oswald was said to have been given a crash course in the Russian language. I have always questioned whether I had been given a subliminal crash course of some type in one or more of the Asian languages. I previously mentioned that when Robert phoned me from California shortly after the Kennedy assassination he had made the statement about my familiarity with an Asian language. I was unaware that I knew any Asian languages and told him so. However, Robert often made statements such as this and I later found them to be true.

I received my Marine Corps discharge in June of 1959 at the Treasure Island Naval base after which I traveled by train back home to Wisconsin. I had intended to return to San Francisco that autumn and enroll in an area college. Tragically, one of my high school friends that I had enlisted with under the buddy program was killed in an auto accident one week after we arrived home. This accident completely changed the course of my life and maybe a fate similar to Oswald's. I enrolled at the La Crosse State Teacher's College in Wisconsin for the fall semester. The MKULTRA had spent a great deal of time and money to train me and turn me into a controlled Marine and I am certain that they did not want to lose me. Other than one phone call from Robert to inquire about my possible return to California, the only contact I had with him was the phone conversation that had taken place shortly after the Kennedy assassination. I have always felt that this was an exploratory phone call to find out if I could recall any past experiences with Oswald and the

MKULTRA. My next contact with Robert had been when I drove to meet him in Madison, WI.

When I visited Robert in California he made a couple of additional comments which took on unusual significance to me. Even though I draw no conclusion to what I am about to write, I must include the experience because of my past, where nothing seems to be what I thought it to be. Again I quote the metaphor; "If it looks like a duck and walks like a duck, it must be a duck." These next two subjects certainly follow that metaphor.

Robert's occupation was caretaker for a section of property that adjoined Esalen Institute. The land that he managed was called Santa Lucia Ranch. It is a small but beautiful parcel of land that rests on cliffs that overlook the Pacific Ocean. Robert explained that the property was owned by a wealthy family from Chicago. He said they were on the board of directors of Esalen Institute and Robert's brother was an attorney in San Francisco law firm that represents the Esalen Institute. I told Robert that I had not heard of Esalen before I arrived at Santa Lucia and he explained that it was a temporary home and school for wayward young women. He mentioned that just the week before he had escorted a young woman back to Esalen that he had seen strolling aimlessly on the road in front of his home. However, a good friend of mine who was an Army officer at Fort Ord in Monterey had a good laugh at my expense when I told him that I had stayed at the Santa Lucia Ranch next to Esalen Institute's home for wayward women. He informed me that Esalen had never functioned in this capacity and I wonder why Robert found it necessary to provide me with disinformation. Because of Robert's lie and our past experience with the CIA and the MKULTRA's mind control program, I immediately began a search for information on the Esalen Institute.

In an article that appeared in *Omni* magazine, Patrick Tierney wrote that, "Esalen is where science and mysticism have been wrestling with each other for 20 years. In that time the institute has established a reputation as the Harvard of the human potential movement. It was home to encounter groups, Gestalt therapy, sports yoga, T'ai Chi, Rolfing, meditation, and massage."

Mark Whitaker, Gerald C. Lubenow, and Joyce Barnathan wrote in an article that appeared in the January 10, 1983, issue of *Newsweek* that, "Esalen has been called "hot-tub diplomacy." As most

> unofficial U.S. Soviet contacts have waned in recent years, one back channel has survived: an unorthodox, informal exchange program developed under the auspices of the Esalen Institute, the Big Sur-based Mecca of the human-potential movement. In the past decade a dozen Esalen enthusiasts have journeyed to the Soviet Union to compare notes on such topics as parapsychology and herbal medicine. Esalen leaders have also invited Soviet scientists and bureaucrats to California.

The author Abraham Maslow called Esalen "potentially the most important educational institution in the world." And in 1978, Rick Tarnas wrote that, "Esalen is a state of

> consciousness as much as it is a physical place. It is a pagan monastery, a school of the mysteries, where seekers of every description come to find light. Breaking out of the crumbling structures of their past, they come to find themselves. At this poignant moment in their lives, Esalen stands like the Temple at Delphi, where paths inward are offered, where they come to discover again their souls, their bodies, their pain, their knowledge, their happiness at being alive. For many, Esalen is where the tide turns in their private revolution against their inner tyrants of the past. Esalen is where the archetypal dimension of reality seems to breathe itself visibly into our world. Somehow the magnificence of its beauty draws out the deep powers of the hu-

man spirit. Esalen is a Kingdom of Death and Rebirth. It is a place inside each of us."

Because Robert-1 and I were mind-controlled by the MKULTRA, I find it interesting that he would be the caretaker at Esalen Institute. I make no link between Esalen Institute, the CIA, and the MKULTRA, but only question if there was, or still is, a connection.

The second of the Roberts interesting comments came as we said farewell after my last visit. He said, "You have to finish your book Hawk; do you realize you are Shibumi?" I had never heard the word Shibumi so I asked him what it meant. He did not define the word but told me to read the book *Shibumi* by Trevanian (the pen name of Rodney William Whitaker).

According to author Trevanian, Shibumi is a Japanese word that's meaning has to do with great refinement underlying commonplace appearances. "It is a statement so correct that it does not

> have to be bold, so poignant it does not have to be pretty, so true it does not have to be real. Shibumi is understanding rather than knowledge. Eloquent silence, in demeanor, it is modesty without pudency. In art, where the spirit of Shibumi takes the form of sabi, it is elegant simplicity, articulate brevity. In philosophy, when Shibumi emerges as wabi, it is spiritual tranquility that is not passive; it is being without the angst of becoming. In the personality of a man, it is authority without domination. How does one achieve Shibumi? One does not achieve it, one discovers it. Only a few men of infinite refinement ever do that, one must pass through knowledge, and arrive at simplicity."

When I arrived home, I purchased the book and read it several times. However, even after several readings, I remained perplexed as to what Robert alluded to with his assertion that I was Shibumi. The Japanese meaning of Shibumi, as Trevanian explained, did not appear to me to be the message that Robert was trying to communicate. I believe the gist of what Robert was trying to convey lies in the content of the story, whereas I had become fixated on the word Shibumi. In the story, the main character, Nicholai Hel, held secrets over the intelligence community as to who killed President John F. Kennedy. I believe, for whatever reason, Robert would not, or could not help or tell me what I needed to know about the Kennedy assassination. He insisted that I continue to pursue the answer and complete this book.

I have no knowledge of what Robert has been involved in the more that 50 years that have passed, but I suspect that he may have been working for the CIA from the time I first met him as a young Marine at Camp Pendleton.

Chapter Nine

Oswald, an Atsugi Marine

I was reading the St. Paul Pioneer Press and was amused by an article that appeared in its sports section. Michelle Wie, a young female professional golfer, was trying to qualify for a men's professional golf tournament. The interviewer asked her why she wanted to golf in a PGA tournament and she said it was something she had always wanted to do ever since she was a young girl. This struck me as being quite ironic as she was just 15 years old at the time.

Likewise, Oswald was only 17 years old when he enlisted in the Marine Corps and had needed his mother's permission and signature to do so. He was merely 20 years old when he supposedly defected to Russia and 24 when he was accused of being the lone assassin of President John F. Kennedy. Where and when did Oswald become this sophisticated spy and motivated Russian defector?

In their book *Oswald Talked,* Ray and Mary La Fontaine assert that the main phases of Oswald's military career, Atsugi and Santa Ana, are focal points of two contrasting interpretations of the Marine. And, both points call for a more complex and socially competent Oswald than the version presented by *Life Magazine* in the aftermath of the assassination.

The first interpretation of Oswald was forged by former Harvard faculty member Edward Jay Epstein and approved by former CIA Chief of Counterintelligence, James Jesus Angleton, whom Epstein cites in his epigraph. This interpretation stems from a question posed by Warren Commission attorneys W. David Slawson and William T. Coleman, Jr. in a top-secret staff report to the Commission: "How are we to assess whether or not what we know of Oswald's 'real life' is not just a 'legend' designed by the KGB and consistently lived out by Oswald there-after?" Epstein said his book

Legend advocated this theory and argued that Oswald was "turned" while in Japan and thereafter acted as a KGB operative.

Unquestionably this was a created legend, not by the KGB when Oswald was in Japan, but by the CIA while Oswald was stationed at Atsugi Naval Air Station (NAS Atsugi) in Japan. It was completed during the many times Oswald was taken from his assigned duties as a radar operator and programmed by the MKULTRA. There is just enough correct information written in *Legend* to confuse the average reader. Because Epstein is a former Harvard faculty member and has an association with the CIA's James J. Angleton, most everything he writes and says is suspect.

Every anniversary of the Kennedy assassination these same organizations crawl out of the woodwork like roaches to dispel any information that may contradict their original findings. Who are these people that at this late date find it necessary to quell any dissent with regards to the original Warren Commission verdict? If we identify these people, their agenda, and who or what motivates them, we will move toward the truth. Methinks they doth protest too much!

It certainly makes very little sense to go back into Oswald's past as the Warren Commission has done to try and prove that he was a lone assassin because of his seemingly disturbed and dysfunctional childhood. Of course, if your agenda is to make the case that he was the lone assassin, any tidbit of information you can conjure up for your rationale is essential. Let's deal with the facts about Oswald and the assassination and not fabricate stories based on circumstances that supposedly stemmed from him having experienced a difficult childhood. If I were one of his family members, I would be very angry at the Warren Commission's characterization of his personality and their concealment of pertinent facts. They revealed that his mother had been married more than once, that he had spent time at a boarding school, and that he had been disciplined for truancy and other childhood discretions. These facts were pointed out in the Warren Commission's report in order to help make sense of the assassination. It was necessary to make Oswald seem dysfunctional by highlighting his less than ideal childhood. With no evidence, the Warren Commission suggested that he also may have been a homosexual. Apparently, they used this to explain his actions as if being a homosexual had anything to do with him being an assassin. During the 1960s, this accusation may have sounded logical to a large segment of the US population, but today it seems absurd. There was some real "stinkin' thinkin'" taking place in the 60s! The Warren Commission wanted the public to accept all of these circumstances as though they would have been a sufficient reason for Oswald to become an assassin.

This following paragraph appears in the Warren Commission Report. "On September 30, 1952,

> Lee enrolled in P.S. 117, a junior high school in the Bronx where the other children apparently teased him because of his "western" clothes and Texas accent. He began to stay away from school, preferring to read magazines and watch television at home by himself. This continued despite the efforts of the school authorities and, to a lesser extent, by his mother to have him return to school. This brings to mind and I must interject here; that I read the great American inventor Thomas Elva Edison was sent home from school as being un-teachable. Truancy charges were brought against Oswald alleging that he was "beyond the control of his mother insofar as school attendance is concerned." Lee Oswald was remanded for psychiatric observation to Youth House, an institution where children are kept for psychiatric observation or for detention pending court appearance or commitment to a child-caring or custodial institution such as a training school. He was in a Youth House from April 16 to May 7, 1953, during which time he was examined by its Chief Psychiatrist, Dr. Renatus Hartogs, and inter-

viewed and observed by other members of the Youth House staff."

Consider that the Warren Commission did not once mention the MKULTRA, but dug up a truancy record from Oswald's childhood. This seems incredible by today's standards as with the prevalence of drugs, gangs, etc., truancy is hardly considered a serious or punishable offense. It seems comparable to the mindset of burning witches and hanging horse thieves. It is interesting to think that Oswald, as a young boy, could not handle ridicule yet just a few years later as a young man withstood the heckling and abuse of a United States Marine Corps drill instructor and graduated from basic training. Oswald achieved what he had always desired, to become a United States Marine. To me, he didn't appear to be a man that could not withstand ridicule.

I joined the Marines with my lifelong friend, Joseph Kurtz, when we were involved in individual combat training at Camp San Onofre on the Camp Pendleton Base. It was thought that Joe was the youngest in the Corps at that time. As the Marines were about to celebrate their birthday, they wanted to feature its youngest and oldest Marines in an article in their *Leatherneck Magazine*. However, they found a Marine younger than Joe who was in basic training in San Diego. That young marine was Lee Harvey Oswald.

In less than one week after the assassination, with Kennedy scarcely placed in his tomb, President Johnson appointed the Warren Commission. The Warren Commission was made up of a group of supposedly "honorable distin-guished men" handpicked by the newly installed President, Lyndon B. Johnson. Johnson pressed the Commission to resolve the assassination and deliver an answer to the American people. All the Warren Commission had to do was make a case against Oswald. The Warren Commission attempted to craft Oswald into an accomplished spy and assassin. They were assisted in this intent by the media and our intelligence community that included the CIA, FBI, and

Naval Intelligence. We must bear in mind that one of the members of the Warren Commission was Allen Dulles the father of the MKULTRA program. Dulles had an ax to grind with Kennedy over his removal of support for the Bay of Pigs invasion in Cuba, which took place under his administration. Shortly before his assassination, President Kennedy had fired Dulles from his post as Director of the CIA. As President, Kennedy made the fatal mistake of thinking that he was calling the "shots," and not the Intelligence Community. Oswald had already been indoctrinated by Dulles' MKULTRA program and would take the fall in the role of a programmed assassin, and claim the title of the patsy.

It has been emphasized that Oswald had always wanted to become a Marine just like his older brother Robert. He received average grades in school, liked his stepfather and loved his mother, was a member of an air patrol unit as a young boy, and did not shirk his military duty. He had a higher than average IQ and memorized the Marine Corps manual before enlisting. He successfully completed basic training, received a top-secret security clearance (which was later stricken from his military records), and worked on the CIA's top-secret U-2 spy plane project while in Japan. And, although this seems quite incredible now, he liked and admired President John F. Kennedy. A rational person would question as to how this forthright young ex-Marine could have become a lone nut assassin.

It was necessary for the Warren Commission to discredit Oswald through character assassination so the American people could believe the report that justified why he killed the president. They made the circumstances fit the situation and seem both factual and plausible. However, why was this character assassination and disinformation necessary? The Warren Commission came up with an answer which is exactly what President Johnson had demanded, truthful or not.

Oswald qualified as a Marksman on the rifle range in basic training. Of course, this is a play on words as it implies he was an excellent shot with a rifle. However, the designation Marksman is the lowest rifle training qualification a Marine can earn next to not qualifying at all. Hollywood movies have made reference to what an expert rifleman Oswald was, but this depiction is just not true. In Basic Training, Oswald would have gone through a variety of intelligence tests and must have achieved high scores in order to have been sent to the Naval Air Technical Training Center in Jacksonville, Florida. Only the brightest Marines qualify for this type of education and there is no doubt that Oswald was a good Marine, if not an exceptional one.

To assist the reader in understanding the movements of Oswald prior to the assassination of President Kennedy, I must emphasize that NAS Atsugi was the Far East headquarters for the CIA and home to its top-secret MKULTRA mind control program. Oswald served a major portion of his tour at Atsugi while on active duty. Much has been said about his difficulty with authority while stationed there and it is likely that Atsugi is where he was first exposed to the MKULTRA program. Any personality changes and authority problems he may have had were manifested at Atsugi. I know this because I am an expert. I was a victim of the same abuse at the same location and at the same point in time.

I believe Gerald Posner's book, *Case Closed*, was published as a disinformation vehicle. Although Posner spliced in facts to make the book credible, it contained misleading information and many errors. Posner made an accurate statement when he reported that one of Oswald's fellow Marines had noted that Oswald's personality had changed after his stay at NAS Atsugi. "He had started to be more aggressive....he took on a new personality, and was now Oswald the man rather than Oswald the rabbit."

While he was stationed at Atsugi, he was placed in the brig for having an unauthorized pistol in his possession.

Oswald had reached inside his locker for shaving cream and accidentally knocked the firearm out where it hit the floor, discharged, and lodged a bullet in his left upper arm. He was sent back to Japan from Taiwan because apparently he emotionally fell apart while on guard duty. The officer who relieved him stated that he was nervous and sobbing because he did not want to be on guard duty any longer. At this point Oswald was losing control and so were his MKULTRA handlers. My guess is that he required further programming. He was sent back to Japan, but not to his former duty station in Atsugi. Instead, he was shipped from Atsugi to a base at Iwakuni situated hundreds of miles away on the island of Honshu. Because he was delivered to Iwakuni, by the Marines, they are culpable in the mind control program. After Oswald returned from Iwakuni, his friends said that he had grown enormously bitter. Once the MKULTRA became involved in Oswald's life, he became a totally different person. While on liberty, he poured a drink over a non-commissioned officer head and tried to pick a fight.

Oswald had been transferred to multiple jobs and locations but spent his final Marine Corps days at the Naval Air Station in El Toro, Santa Ana, CA. These movements and reassignments gave the MKULTRA plenty of time to work with him. As he did not have to report to any particular duty section for a period of time, no one would know or perhaps care where he was or what happened to him and would not rouse concern among his friends. This is exactly the same procedure that was used on me at Atsugi. I was moved about in the same manner at the same point in time. I had been transferred from mess duty, to guard duty, and then to teletype school in Iwakuni. I traveled with the Marine Air Wing to Taiwan where I was transferred from a non-commissioned officer in charge of the headquarters message center with a top-secret clearance, to a guard unit as a military policeman.

If Oswald were the sophisticated spy and assassin as he is often depicted, he became this individual after he entered the Marine Corps. Bear in mind that he was just 17 years old when he enlisted and 20 when he was discharged from the Marine Corps and traveled to the Soviet Union. In my judgment there is no question as to whether or not Oswald was a victim of the MKULTRA that performed its devious work in Atsugi. It is obvious that when he arrived at Atsugi he was neither a sophisticated spy nor a lone nut. At what point did this transformation take place? I maintain the transformation occurred while he was stationed at Atsugi. This is when the MKULTRA took him, along with other unsuspecting young Marines, and used them as guinea pigs in their mind control games to try and create a perfect Manchurian Candidate. This seems to be just an evolution of the MKULTRA's Nazi Party beginnings in Germany.

In his book *The Search for Lee Harvey Oswald*, author Robert J. Groden tells of a young man who entered the office of New Orleans District Attorney Edward Gillen in 1963. The young man asked Gillen if he knew anything about the legality of importing a new drug known as LSD into the United States. He said he had a source for LSD and wanted to know if it might be illegal. This discussion took place in October of 1963 and Gillen thought he had been visited by a crank. However, while watching television the day after the Kennedy assassination Gillen was startled to see that Oswald had been arrested and charged in the murderer of President Kennedy. Oswald had been the young man that had visited him.

In 1963, one of the only known sources for LSD was the CIA. It had been experimenting with LSD in its Project Artichoke program that was the Agency's first Manchurian Candidate experiment. The program dated back to 1951 when the CIA performed experiments at two overseas military installations in the 1960's. One of these sites was NAS Atsugi. In these experiments, off duty Marines were regularly fed mescaline, sodium pentothal, depressants, amphetamines, and LSD. One of these unsuspecting Marines was Kerry Thornley who stated, "It was pretty weird. I'm eighteen at the time and chasing all the whores in town, and the CIA guys are buying my drinks and paying for the whores and giving me a whole lot of drinks with lots of weird drugs in them. Pretty soon all the shadows are moving around, we're in this bar, see and samurais are everywhere, and I started to see skeletons and things. My mind just started boiling over going about a thousand miles a minute. I'm sure there are going to be some little ladies who're gonna be surprised that illegal drugs like heroin and LSD were freely used by government agents. But, that was just the way it was."

It is strange that only a few Marines remember Oswald occasionally getting drunk. If true, these were the only times in his life he ever drank. Almost everyone who knew him, both before and after his enlistment, including his wife Marina, said that he was a non-drinker. Over the many years since the assassination, Oswald has been greatly maligned by the Warren Commission and the news media. Because his story has been so distorted over the years it is very difficult to view him as a victim. However, Oswald was indeed a victim although media propaganda describes him as a dysfunctional lone-nut assassin, a traitor, and a defector. And although that character assassination was not sufficient enough, the government changed his Marine Corps honorable discharge to an undesirable discharge. What more could they do to chastise him?

What a travesty of justice these people perpetuated who were in the position of power over this young man whose only wish was to be a good Marine. It pleases me to know that his mother, Marguerite, always knew and believed in her son's innocence and knew he was not guilty of the charges brought against him. She always maintained that he was a government agent and worked for the intelligence community. The honorable men on the Warren Commission portrayed Marguerite as a harebrained woman, yet she was absolutely correct in her accusations. Oswald's family should be made aware and understand that he was innocent of the charges brought against him by the Warren Commission and the media. Consequently, Oswald performed only those duties for which he was controlled and programmed to perform. Indeed, he was the patsy he professed to be, and obviously one of the few individuals in Dallas that day that expressed the truth.

It is my conviction that Oswald did not murder anyone, nor did he make an attempt on General Edwin A. Walker's life prior to the Kennedy assassination despite the Warren Commission's assertion that he was a Marksman Marine and that he shot President Kennedy from a sixth story window as his limousine cruised past. The supposed attempt on General Walker's life was made at night while he sat seated at his desk in front of a window in his home. Allegedly, Oswald shot and missed; the bullet passing near Walker's head. Purportedly, Oswald became very frightened and panicked, hid the rifle, and ran home and told his wife Marina what he had done. However, there is absolutely no evidence to link Oswald to the General Walker shooting incident. According to a Dallas police report, an attempt on the General's life was made on April 10, 1963. Someone had taken a shot at General Walker through his window on that night and although there is no concrete evidence linking Oswald to the shooting, the Warren Commission still found it necessary to implicate Oswald in this crime. If, through circumstantial evidence, the Warren Commission can alter the facts and link him to deviant and other criminal acts, then there takes very little stretch of the imagination in turning him into an assassin.

In the book *Oswald Talked,* authors Ray and Mary La Fontaine assert that there appears to be an alternate version of Oswald's activities and this may be acquired from the Marines who knew him best at MACS-9 in El Toro. The significance of their observations is that Oswald was neither the lone Marxist rube of Life Magazine, nor the KGB operative of author Epstein's opinion. The MACS-9 Oswald was actually fixated on Cuba; seemingly as an intelligence agent who occasionally tried to recruit other Marines for some US Federal agency.

According to MACS-9 Marine Bud Simco, Oswald was generally sloppy, wore his hat down over his eyes "Beetle-

Bailey" style, kept his boots scuffed, and almost seemed to cultivate an unkempt appearance." As a result, says Simco, "anytime a work detail was formed, he was usually the first to be selected. He would take everything in stride with a "cocky so what' attitude," and was never seen to lose his cool or "be particularly upset by anything."

While at El Toro and attached to MACS-9, Oswald roomed with Jim Anthony Botelho of San Juan Bautista, CA, who later became a judge. The men became friends and Botelho invited Oswald to his home in San Juan Bautista for the weekend where Oswald met his family. The La Fontaine's write that according

to Simco, when Oswald hastily applied for an early discharge on grounds of family hardship, Jim and everyone else in the company was surprised to learn that the request was granted so quickly. During the day that Oswald awaited the discharge, he made "quite a few trips" back to MACS-9 to visit his friend Botelho, repeatedly telling him of the discharge and about going to Cuba, where he would be paid to train troops. Oswald seemed to be trying to recruit his listeners to volunteer for such a venture. Botelho begged off, saying he knew nothing about training troops and anyway "was a lover, not a fighter." To such objections Oswald reportedly replied that they could "fake it." Oswald "made this suggestion more than once and was serious, but no one seemed interested."

Later, when the MACS-9 Marines finally learned of Oswald's defection to Russia, several of those who knew him, including Simco and Botelho, speculated that he was on a mission for the US government and not a genuine defector. Today a Justice of the Peace, Botelho still strongly believes that Oswald traveled to the Soviet Union as a US agent and that he was essentially a "gentle man" and a "pacifist" who would not have murdered the president. "I will never believe that," he says. "If he was involved, it was as an informant of some kind, someone who was probably trying to stop the assassination, not participate in it. He was a hero of our time, not a killer."

Oswald did not forward top-secret information to the Soviet Union which gave them the ability to shoot down our top-secret U-2 spy plane. Whatever circumstances which Oswald may have been implicated of having performed, it was solely because he was being controlled by the MKULTRA.

In his book *Conspiracy*, Anthony Summers writes that intelligence involvement in the assassination remains an open question. A staff investigator told him that in particular

> "the Military Intelligence angle was not covered adequately and the Defense Department held out on us, and that after all it is the department that destroyed the Oswald file. A number of clues suggest that before the assassination, Oswald was a tool of some part of American intelligence. (Describing Oswald as a tool is quite accurate.) Such disturbing leads demand urgent further inquiry. Nobody I spoke to on the Assassinations Committee, whatever his personal opinion on the evidence, felt that the case had yet been exhaustively investigated. All agree that lack of time and funds forced the Committee to leave important research unfinished. What an injustice to both the Kennedy and Oswald families that in solving the assassination it was reduced

down to not an adequate amount of time to find the real killers."

The Warren Commission does not mention Oswald's supposed involvement in the downing of the top-secret U-2 spy plane that caused an international incident. However, it goes to great lengths to connect Oswald to the Fair Play for Cuba Committee in New Orleans. The Commission never mentioned that he was the only member in New Orleans and that the Fair Play for Cuba office which was located across the street from the CIA office.

The MKULTRA program should have been thoroughly researched by the Warren Commission as former CIA Director Allen Dulles was one of its members. During the same point in time that Oswald was being controlled by the MKULTRA, Dulles served as CIA director and was a founder of the mind control program that operated at NAS Atsugi. Gerald Patrick Hemming, Roscoe White, and Kerry Thornley were all stationed at NAS Atsugi along with Oswald and all were involved in the Dealey Plaza mix in Dallas. Interestingly, only Thornley was interviewed by the Warren Commission. It is very unusual as to why there is no mention of the mind control program that may have caused Oswald's unusual behavior, but much has been written about the attempted assassination of General Walker with no proof of any Oswald connection. The Warren Commission spent a large part of their research on Oswald's childhood and how it affected him and shaped him into becoming a dysfunctional adult and assassin. As I previously stated, there is no mention of the CIA mind control program that was operating at NAS Atsugi while Oswald was stationed there.

I first met Oswald while I served on mess duty at Atsugi. We were not close friends, only fellow Marines, two men among a few hundred on the small base. I recall talking with Oswald while I was head counter at the entry to the mess hall. My job was to stand outside the mess hall door to keep the chow line orderly and count the number of Marines that passed through for their meal. Oswald was always pleasant and a bit cocky or perhaps even a bit arrogant, but often that goes hand in hand with being a Marine. We would often share small talk while he waited his turn in line. I would also see him periodically outside the mess hall as his barracks was located across the street from mine. He was referred to as an officer baiter; a person who antagonizes an officer through verbal poking and prodding. I also enjoyed the officer baiting game, but was careful to mind the limits as to how far one can prod and poke and still stay free from trouble.

In the book *The Man Who Knew Too Much*, author Dick Russell writes that Richard Case Nagell, a former commissioned officer in the US Army, performed duties as an intelligence officer for the CIA in the Far East along with his regular duties with the Counter Intelligence Corp (CIC). The CIC operated in the Far East at the time Oswald and I were stationed at Atsugi. Nagell had been instructed never to mention the phrase Field Operations Intelligence or its acronym FOI outside of a secure place or in the presence of unauthorized persons; it was not to be used even around headquarters. Russell writes that the FOI was subordinate and operationally responsible to the Army's Office of the Assistant Chief of Staff for Intelligence. However, FOI was merely an augmentation to CIA special military operations, a covert extension of CIA policy and activity designed to conceal the true nature of CIA objectives. A substantial portion of FOI's financial support came from the CIA, directly or through reimbursement, as did much of its technological support. A number of FOI operations in which I participated, or about which I gained knowledge, were closely associated with or directed by the CIA. Russell states in his many books that he had read about the CIA and Military Intelligence while researching to try and find something on Field Operations Intelligence (FOI). In his research, he came across only a single reference that appeared in the book *The Secret War: The story of interna-*

tional espionage since 1945 written in 1962 by Sanche de Gramont (Ted Morgan). It appeared in a section describing the links between the CIA and the military's Counter Intelligence Corps (CIC) branch in West Germany.

The CIC's main objective was to find Communist agents in US military installations, such as clerical or kitchen help, and help to sift agents who came to West Berlin as refugees. Agents thus found were turned over to the CIA for possible use as double agents. Army Intelligence in West Germany also has an operational espionage group, the mysterious Field Operations Intelligence (FOI). The CIA trumps all other agencies and takes over any case it chooses to handle. Victor Marchetti a retired CIA officer and author of the book *The CIA and the Cult of Intelligence,* confirmed the existence of an organization such as the FOI operating in Japan, and quite possibly at Atsugi.

Nagell identified to Russell the names of the two commanding officers that had worked for the FOI in the Far East. They were found in the directory of the Association of Former Intelligence Officers and were listed as John B. Stanley and Robert C. Roth. The two men verified they had been the top two officials of the FOI. Colonel Stanley told Russell that he had commanded FOI from the end of 1954 until the beginning of 1960. Stanley said the FOI worked independent of the CIC and that the FOI collected intelligence in denied areas. It is interesting to note that it was at this same time period that Oswald was in Atsugi. Perhaps they could have been his handlers? Anyone considered unfriendly was a target, and they were particularly interested in North Korea, China, and the Soviet Union. According to Stanley, the area the FOI covered extended from the North Pole to the borders of India and Hawaii to the Ural Mountains. He also mentioned that he did not think it was a secret any longer and they had some Japanese fishermen that would travel to the coast of the Soviet Union and fill them in with any information they may find. Most of the information gathered regarded ports, as the FOI's primary mission was to gather intelligence on early warning signals or troop size.

Stanley said his unit consisted of at least 75 to 80 officers, and somewhere between 1,500 and 2,000 enlisted men. He was not quite sure of the size as they had units in various places in Japan as well as a unit in Korea, units in the Philippines, Bangkok, and especially in Taiwan, where the Nationalist Chinese were very cooperative. He noted that in Taiwan they were allowed to place people undercover. He thought this was the first time this had been tried; taking men out of uniform and getting them civilian jobs.

Marquis Williams Childs told Russell that he had been attached to the US Embassy in Tokyo as the FBI's man between 1954 and 1967, and then again from 1969 through 1976. Childs stated he handled a large variety of security cases and trying to guard against what hostile countries might be doing against us back in the United States.

The previous paragraphs explain to a degree what may have been my reason for traveling to Yokohama almost every weekend and why I would end up in the same restaurant, not able to recall anything. I was obviously a mind controlled courier but I have no idea what I may have delivered. In the previous chapter I detailed the day that my friend Robert and I spent in an aboriginal village in the mountains of Taiwan. The village was extremely remote and the perfect location for a secret military rendezvous. It was very unusual for us to have seen Oswald there. Although Robert and I were accompanied by our friends from the Chinese military, Oswald appeared to be alone. I often wonder how he came to be there that day, especially if you consider his activity timeline and the fact that he should have been in Japan. It is quite mysterious how this young low-ranking Marine traveled from Japan to Taiwan without military permission and assistance. Was he under the control of the MKULTRA and used as a courier?

I have given much thought as to why there were no other Americans on the excursion and have concluded that we had been infiltrated by either Nationalist or Communist Chinese military intelligence. Either there was a mole within the CIA or we were working with the Chinese as it was doubtful that the CIA would have gone to such lengths to acquire information. Normally, the CIA would merely request information from Naval Intelligence through the chain of command. It is quite possible that we were working as couriers for the Republic of China and delivering messages from within our headquarters.

Let's not automatically accept the conclusion submitted to us by the honorable men on the Warren Commission that Oswald is guilty of killing President Kennedy. Instead, let's approach the assassination with an open mind and presume that Oswald is innocent until proven guilty. Let's also accept the likelihood that Oswald was under someone else's control when we move toward a conclusion. We should approach the assassination in this manner as opposed to using some type of unusual behavior based on Oswald's overblown childhood problems the Warren Commission would have us believe. Only if you understand and accept that Oswald was programmed and controlled, will his seemingly unusual behavior take on a completely new connotation.

If Oswald manifested serious behavior problems because of a dysfunctional childhood, he would not have been accepted for enlistment nor been able to withstand Marine Corps basic training. The Warren Commission portrayed him as being a dangerous and fanatical communist; however, this behavior must have been developed while he was a Marine. In the Corps, you are trained to live, breath, and think like a Marine and to become a member of an elite fighting force. You have little time to develop an individual personality within this structured environment. The USMC is proud to let everyone know about this transformation and their recruitment ads boast, "The few. The Proud. The Marines." Many have heard the familiar saying, "Once a Marine, always a Marine." And when fellow Marines greet one another they use the term "Semper Fi" which is an abbreviated form of the Latin term, "Semper Fidelis" or "Always Faithful". Oswald became one of the few, proud, and always faithful, but his government failed him. The Corps took this young man and played with his mind. In his book *Oswald's Tale: An American Mystery*, Norman Mailer wrote that for Americans, the most astonishing aspect of Oswald's defection was that he had been a Marine and Marines do not defect, they plant flags on Iwo Jima.

Let us follow Oswald, beginning with his hardship discharge from the Marine Corps in September of 1959. Then follow his movements, which will take on new meaning and understanding now that you recognize he was being controlled by the MK ULTRA.

I have neither the expertise nor the resources to have gathered all of the following information that I am about to reveal to you, so I will use information gleaned from such superb research books as *Oswald and The CIA*, by John Newman; *Killing the Truth* by Harrison Edward Livingstone; *The Search for The Manchurian Candidate* by John Marks; *Best Evidence* by David Lifton; *The Man Who Knew to Much* by Dick Russell; *Plausible Denial* by Mark Lane; *Conspiracy* by Anthony Summers; *Bloody Treason* by Noel Twyman; and *Whitewash* by Harold Weisberg, the book that started the questioning of the Warren Commission report. I have also used information gathered from numerous newspaper and magazine articles that I have researched over the past 44 years. Finally, I use my own knowledge and personal experience of having been a controlled Manchurian Candidate Marine and my contact with Oswald as we both were products of the MKULTRA's mind control program and used as guinea pigs while serving at NAS Atsugi.

My objective is to illustrate the control the MKULTRA had over Oswald's movements, thoughts, and actions. Previously, I mentioned that it is possible that Oswald,

Robert, and I were controlled at one point in time by the Chinese military intelligence. There would have had to have been involvement and complicity by other intelligence agencies in the United States government, such as Naval Intelligence and the FBI which enabled the CIA to operate unrestricted, thereby placing us in the Dragon's Den. I maintain that rogue units within the CIA are the real culprits in the assassination of President Kennedy and the sabotage of the top-secret U-2 spy plane.

Oswald's programming began at Atsugi, Japan, the CIA headquarters in the Far East. The Agency controlled and manipulated his movements while he was in the Soviet Union and in the US while he was in New Orleans and Dallas. If one is to understand Oswald, a person must look beyond and not accept the constructed personality profile that the Warren Commission and others have manufactured for him. They must take a different view. This new information should leave little doubt as to whether Oswald was guilty of assassinating the President, or was merely a controlled patsy.

The Warren Commission would like to have it both ways as they depict Oswald as weak and a mama's boy. Oswald is portrayed as being overly dependent on his mother almost to the extent that he could not function on his own. Yet while in the service, he was quite self-sufficient and sent home a portion of his payroll to her each month to assist with living expenses. Then suddenly, a few months before he completed his tour of duty, he applied for and was granted an early discharge. This is very unusual behavior when, according to the Warren Commission, Oswald had applied for an overseas extension while serving at NAS Atsugi. This request was denied based on an episode that took place one night while Oswald was on liberty. As I mentioned earlier, he was charged with having a heated argument with a non-commissioned officer and poured a drink over him. This incident happened in the Bluebird Bar just outside the base. Bluebird was the code name for the MKULTRA program and the Bluebird Bar is where the CIA played many of their mind control games on unsuspecting young Marines.

After arriving back in the US from Japan, Oswald took a 30-day leave and went back to Fort Worth, Texas, to stay with his mother. When he returned to complete his tour of duty and muster out of the Marine Corps, he was then stationed at El Toro Marine Air Base in Santa Anna, CA. According to most Marines interviewed by the Warren Commission, it was during this time that he spoke almost continuously about Russia. It is thought by researchers that he spent time at the Defense Language Institute (DLI) in Monterey and was given a crash course in Russian. It is believed that DLI had had developed a technique to teach a foreign language in an accelerated and subliminal format. I am certain that my missing weekend spent in Monterey was at the DLI and have fragmented memories of a clinical or hospital atmosphere.

It was at El Toro Marine Base where Oswald met Kerry Thornley and Nelson Delgado who were fellow Marines that were questioned by the Warren Commission. Thornley maintained that he had been mind controlled by the MKULTRA while he was stationed in the Far East. What is also strange is that Kerry Thornley met Oswald at El Toro after his return from Atsugi, after which Thornley was transferred to Atsugi. Oswald's commanding officer during this time, Lt. John E. Donavan, also gave testimony before the Warren Commission. In the Delgado's testimony, he mentioned a man that Oswald met outside the main gate at El Toro. And in later testimony by Patrick Gerald Hemming, he revealed to the Warren Commission that he had been that individual. Hemming had also been at Atsugi during the time Oswald was stationed there. I will discuss in detail Gerald Patrick Hemming and how he is involved in the conspiracy.

An early discharge is accomplished in a variety of ways and Oswald chose a hardship discharge that allowed him to return home to help his mother who required living assistance. She had been injured at work when a can of candy had fallen off a shelf and landed on the bridge of her nose. She acquired the necessary papers from her doctor, lawyers, and friends to certify her disability. Thus Oswald was granted the early hardship discharge and traveled home to Fort Worth, TX. He arrived home, stayed one day and left again without warning. He explained to his mother and brother that he was in the import-export business and needed to travel to Europe. The next time his family had contact with him he was in the Soviet Union where he supposedly renounced his citizenship and requested permanent residence. His brother Robert said he did not know Oswald was in Russia until October 31, 1959, when he read about his arrival in the newspaper. It seems odd that Oswald had not told Robert of his defection as it has been confirmed he was preparing to defect for two years and was not planning to return to the US again for any reason. This certainly does not sound like the behavior of a young "Mama's boy" who had recently been granted a hardship discharge to return home to assist his mother.

In a note to his mother Oswald's wrote, "I have booked passage on a ship to Europe. I would have had to sooner or later and I think its best I go now just remember above all else that my values are different from Robert's or yours. It is difficult to tell you how I feel. Just remember this is what I must do. I did not tell you about my plans because you could hardly be expected to understand." The following is a letter that Oswald sent to Robert just before leaving Russia for his return trip to the United States.

Dear Robert,

This will be the last letter you get from us from the USSR.

In case you hear about our coming or the newspapers hear about it (I hope they won't), I want to warn you not to make any comments whatsoever about me. None at all!!! I know what was said about me when I left the U.S. as Mother sent me some clippings from the newspapers, however. I realize that it was just the news which made you say all those things. However, I'll just remind you again not to make any statements or comments if you are approached by the newspapers between now and the time we actually arrive in the U.S.

Hope to see you soon, Love to the family.

Your brother,

Lee

This certainly does not sound like the man that the Warren Commission and the media portrayed, or the man that left the US to denounce his citizenship. It is as though the men are two different individuals. And, I think in reality, there really were two Oswalds; the 'real' one, and the MKULTRA programmed Oswald.

When they first heard of the assassination, the majority of the people in Russia who knew Oswald immediately said that Alik (Oswald) could not have committed the crime. The following are comments and quotes from his Russian friends that appeared in the book *Oswald's Tale, An American Mystery*, by the author Norman Mailer.

Rimma: She felt that Alik was somehow connected with the crime but, never killed the American President.

Sasha: Her impression of Oswald was that he could never have assassinated Kennedy. "He is a person who would not kill a fly."

Pavel: He was offended when the Warren Commission depicted Oswald as an underdeveloped mentality. He was very offended and didn't like the idea that somebody who was not stupid, was being shown to the whole world as if he were. Mailer writes that Pavel collected all kinds of different articles on the subject and could never accept it as fact. However, as he read more and more, he decided that one person could always make another do anything. You can certainly change a person by force. In Pavel's opinion, Oswald was not Kennedy's murderer, but was somehow involved in a plot. Because, after all, Oswald is no angel.

Anatoly: "Somebody kills somebody and then is killed in two days; it's very dubious if he really did it. There is somebody un-accused who is guilty. It's very negative to me."

Ilya: "Oswald never talked much about the assassination except to say it was organized. Killing President Kennedy was organized. If they had used Alik, it was because he had been in the Soviet Union."

Ella: Asked whether she thought Alik was guilty, she could not believe the possibility, "He was so gentle."

Igor Ivanovich: "Lee was the scum of society, a person spoiled from the cradle, so to say, not serious, inconstant. Something was probably wrong with his state of mind." Ivanovich also stated that you could not find one single person from Minsk who would say that Oswald had intentions to go back to America and cause all of that trouble.

Stepan Vasilyevich: When he heard of the announcement on the radio he thought "It is impossible!" As news arrived from various broadcasts, he came to the conclusion that Oswald could not have done it alone. He believed that he had been sucked into it somehow, because the single fact that he had been in the Soviet Union was being exploited. Vasilyevich also commented that if Oswald had been CIA, he could not have done any more in Minsk than gather information in a contemplative way, not manifesting anything, as he was not an active agent.

However, in his book, Mailer misses something that almost all researchers also fail to recognize; Oswald was controlled. These individuals persist in trying to explain the many inconsistencies in his life, but it can't be done. Both Mailer and the Warren Commission went as far as to tag him as a latent homosexual to explain his curious and unpredictable actions. As if curious and unpredictable actions define homosexuality. Oswald's inconsistencies were caused solely by the fact he was a subject of the MKULTRA program, and therefore was a controlled agent that performed their misdeeds. He reverted back to his natural personality when left alone; the personality that his family and Russian friends had known. This is why they could not believe that he was capable of committing such a horrendous crime. But when Oswald was controlled by the MKULTRA, he became someone else operating as a Manchurian Candidate. Consequently, he would appear to have a split personality, but once you realize that he was not in control of his behavior, a new understanding of his unpredictable character is revealed.

The CIA used Oswald as a decoy so that he would be implicated in the act of passing along information to the Russians. The public was informed that this information made it possible for the Russian's to shoot down the U-2 spy plane. As this incident caused international embarrassment for the US, the CIA pointed their dirty finger at Oswald. However, Oswald's commanding officer at El Toro stated that all aircraft call signs, codes, and radar frequencies were changed once it was known that he was in Russia. And, it was normal operating procedure to change these codes and signals on a monthly basis. This incident was the first time Oswald was used as a patsy. Oswald did nothing wrong and did not denounce his citizenship. He continued on with his life and married a Russian girl. He returned to the US to be manipulated by the MKULTRA for another mission not yet planned. The Oswald legend was almost complete. The downing of the U-2 kept the Cold War chugging along while the military establishment reaped the rewards. In his farewell address, President Eisenhower expressed his fears in the military establishment when he stated, "we must guard against the acquisition of unwarranted influence whether sought or unsought, by the military industrial complex. The potential for the disastrous rise of misplaced power exists and will persist."

Oswald traveled from New Orleans to Le Havre, France, aboard the SS Marion Lykes and traveled on to England where he flew to Helsinki, Finland, but it is not known how he then made his way to Russia. I question where he obtained the money necessary for this expensive trip and how he achieved clearance to visit the countries. There has been continuous debate on how he obtained his visa to enter the Soviet Union and many speculate that the KGB had arranged for his entry. Mailer stated that it is almost irrelevant how Oswald arrived in the Soviet Union and I find this comment surprising because if he was assisted by either the CIA or the KGB, our understanding of his motive for traveling to Russia will also change. We do know that Oswald had applied for a Visa to enter the Soviet Union while in Helsinki where it could be obtained quickly and easily. But how could he have known this unless it had been planned by someone else? Supposedly, this was well known information to insiders, but Oswald was not an insider. When we recall that Oswald was a very young man at this point, how did he acquire the knowledge, freedom and determination to travel unassisted to Russia by an unconventional route through Helsinki? Additionally, the trip would have been expensive and he was most certainly on a limited salary as a low-ranked enlisted Marine who sent money to his mother every month and gave her $100 before he left for Russia. ($100 at this time was greater than one month's military salary.) As quoted by Norman Mailer, author Edward Epstein noted that it was possible that Oswald was engaged on the periphery of espionage. He made a close calculation of what it would have cost Oswald to travel to Moscow against what he had saved in the Marine Corps, and ended with the estimate that was not enough to account for the deluxe arrangements Oswald had purchased. There appeared to be a shortfall of at least $500 and the possibility cannot be ignored that he made up the difference by selling information in Japan. There is some indication that he was also selling information in Los Angeles.

Philip Melanson, Dartmouth professor and coordinator of the Robert F. Kennedy Archive, stated that the CIA claimed it had no interest in Oswald and did not debrief him upon his return from Russia. Melanson, who wrote *Spy Saga: Lee Harvey Oswald and U.S. Intelligence*, stated that Oswald proved himself to be a rather keen observer of the things around him. Back in Dallas a fellow worker remembers his commenting that the Soviet disbursement of military units was different from the US pattern: the Soviets did not intermingle their armor and infantry divisions, but would place all their aircraft in one location and all their infantry in another. Melanson noted, "These are curious interests for a befuddled young ideologue. With an eye for detail like that it is indeed a shame that the CIA missed talking to him." Was the CIA so simple-minded that it saw no possible connection between Oswald and the U-2 incident? Did the CIA already know precisely what Oswald had told the Soviets?

In *Perfect Assassin*, author Jerry Leonard wrote that there were several peculiar facts surrounding Oswald's defection and his theory is that this defection was related to the U-2 spy plane program. "Curiously, the day Oswald reached Moscow, the high-level Russian intelligence

agent who had warned of leaks involving the U-2 spy plane program was arrested by the Soviets. Also of interest, while Oswald was still in Russia a U-2 pilot named Gary Powers was shot down over the USSR while on a reconnaissance mission. This mission which flew over the Soviet Union was only the second flight over the USSR following Oswald's defection. Powers later blamed Oswald who had been trained to track these planes as a radar technician at the Atsugi base in Japan, and for providing the soviets with enough information to track and destroy his plane. In a final irony, following his homecoming to the US, Oswald the supposed Marxist would be employed by a Dallas graphic arts Company that performed classified work for the Army Map Service that used photos generated by spy planes such as the U-2."

Why do so many researchers and official government agencies keep walking away from the obvious? When you do not involve the CIA in the assassination equation, you then have to speculate on entirely different results. In the *Memoirs of Sherlock Holmes*, Sir Arthur Conan Doyle writes, "It is one of those instances where the reasoner can produce an effect which seems remarkable to his neighbor, because the latter has missed the one little point which is the basis of the deduction." Let's keep it simple, Lee Harvey Oswald was a Manchurian Candidate.

In the book *Perfect Assassin*, Jerry Leonard wrote that in the same year that Oswald defected to Russia, the FBI, in conjunction with the Pentagon, recruited another low-level military man to serve as a "dangle" to the Soviets. The code name for this plan was Operation Shocker in which the US intelligence community desired to gather information about the Soviet's nerve gas program. They wanted to mislead them into taking research paths the US had already investigated and found unusable in order for them to waste time and money. This operation lasted more than 20 years; the FBI lured the Soviets into recruiting an American soldier as a spy so that the US could artfully use him as a double agent for disinformation and counter espionage purposes. The FBI also wanted to give the Soviets faulty information regarding a germ warfare agent the US had abandoned. Under the code name SHOCKER, there was another top-secret program named WALLFLOWER that provided an agent with classified documents to be given to the Soviets in hopes it would convince them of the agent's legitimacy. This program was run by the Army and FBI who selected a serviceman to be dangled to the Russians. The FBI would run the agent and the Army would feed the agent false classified material. Within the Pentagon, an elaborate system of secret panels reviewed the information to be released. Ultimately, the Joint Chiefs of Staff approved the documents given to the Russians. The double agent was recruited in 1959 from a pool of US military personal stationed in Japan.

The continuous battle against communism was pervasive in 1958 and especially during the time I was stationed in Taiwan. On R&R in Hong Kong, we were instructed that it was a court marshal offence to purchase anything that had been made in the Republic of China. It was during this same time period that Oswald traveled to the Soviet Union. Technically, he was still a Marine and subject to recall as he would have been on inactive reserve status for three years following his hardship discharge. Amazingly, he traveled with no complications and entered Russia directly into the eye of the communist storm that existed at that time.

John A. McVickar, second consul at the American Embassy in Moscow, told the State Department in 1964 that Oswald would have had to make a direct and completely arranged trip. Oswald had been discharged from the Marine Corps in September of 1959 and had arrived in Moscow in October of 1959. His stop in Helsinki was an ideal place to acquire a quick entry Visa. Helsinki was a well known entry point among people who are working in the Soviet Union and undoubtedly people who are associated with Soviet matters. At a later date McVickar told the Warren Commission; "I would say it was not a commonly known fact among the ordinary run of people in the United States." At the time, the average turn-around time for a Visa in Helsinki was still 7 to 14 days. The Warren Commission had supposedly researched this point very carefully and noted that if travel exceptions were made, it was done in Helsinki. Oswald would have required assistance in order to arrive in Helsinki to receive an expedited Visa. That fact that he successfully obtained his Visa without complications suggests that his defection had been well planned and intended to be completed very quickly.

Upon his arrival in Moscow, Oswald went to the American Embassy where he met Richard Snyder, the American Consul. The day he arrived there, another American was also there; a graduate student named Ned Keenan who lived in Leningrad. Keenan made the statement that he thought Oswald looked unusual and that he was a memorable character and strangely dressed. Snyder recalled that it was a chilly October morning but Oswald was dressed in jeans, had no coat or hat, and wore thin white dress gloves. I would assume these would have been the white military gloves that are part of a Marine's dress blue uniform. Snyder was intrigued by the humorless and robotic demeanor of Oswald. A young girl who had been visiting her mother in the office remarked, "Mommy who was that weird man at your desk?" The robotic humorless demeanor that Snyder mentions indicates a form of control. I know there was nothing weird or unusual about Oswald when he was a Marine at Atsugi, so why would a young girl describe him as such a few months later?

Oswald was called to Snyder's desk where he came to attention. This is odd behavior for a man who is about to denounce his citizenship and who, according to The Warren Commission, despised authority. When Snyder asked how he could help him, Oswald replied, "I've come to give up my American passport and renounce my citizenship." Oswald then handed him a note that formally announced his intention to defect to the Soviet Union. He also commented that he had thought it over very carefully and that he knew what he was doing. He stated that he had recently been discharged from the Marine Corps and had been planning the defection for years. He maintained that he knew what he was doing and did not want any lectures or advice. Oswald said, "Lets save my time and yours, and you just give me the papers to sign and I'll leave." The papers he referred to were the necessary forms to formally renounce American citizenship. Snyder said he was surprised by Oswald's cocksure and arrogant attitude and that he felt this was part of a planned speech he had rehearsed before entering the Embassy. I think that Oswald had help from the MKULTRA in the preparation of this speech. It is easy to be confident when you know that you have the support of the CIA and US government behind you.

Snyder said that Oswald had tried to remain calm during their encounter but that he was wound up tighter than a clock spring. He told Snyder that he had not applied for a Soviet tourist Visa until he reached Helsinki on October 14. He also stated that he had purposefully informed the Russian Embassy of his intention to stay in the country permanently. He mentioned that he had written a letter to the Supreme Soviet Consul on October 16 in which he requested a citizenship application. Snyder checked Oswald's passport and discovered that he was a 20-year-old ex-Marine; a minor. He told him that he would need additional information and requested his home address in Texas as it had been scratched off his passport. He also requested to know his closest living relative and Oswald became very upset at the thought of his mother being involved. However, he was forthcoming with the address. He mentioned that he wanted to become a Marxist and that the matter should be handled quickly. He warned Snyder that he was wise to the fact that he may try to talk him out of defecting. This statement suggests that he was prompted on what was going to happen during his visit. Because Oswald had not revealed that he was going to defect, who coached him through this process? During the interview, Snyder asked Oswald if he was willing to serve the Soviet State. Oswald replied that while enlisted he had been a radar operator and that he had voluntarily stated to unnamed Soviet officials that he would reveal information concerning the Marine Corps and details of his special training. He declared that he might know something of special interest. It is curious as to why Oswald would choose to reveal this information if he was trying to be processed through the Embassy as quickly as possible. One must wonder what special information Oswald carried that would have been of special interest beyond his military and radar operator knowledge.

McVickar noted that Oswald informed them he was going to turn over classified information to the Russians. Of course, neither Snyder nor McVickar were privy to the top-secret U-2 spy plane housed at NAS Atsugi. Consequently, they would have had no idea as to what Oswald meant. Snyder and McVickar assumed that Oswald thought the Embassy had been bugged by the KGB because he spoke as if he were speaking directly to the organization. Snyder testified before The Warren Commission that he thought it was peculiar and extraordinary act for anyone to walk into an American Embassy anywhere in the world, let alone Moscow at the height of the Cold War, and to announce, in the presence of American consular officials, one's intent to commit a deliberate act of espionage. This fact bears asking the question that if Oswald was a CIA agent or a Manchurian-type courier, why he would have mentioned the U-2 program at the same time that President Eisenhower denied its existence. I believe he mentioned it to keep the Cold War rolling along so that the American military complex could continue to prosper. I believe it is incredibly bizarre that Oswald's sole purpose at the Embassy was to denounce his United States citizenship, and yet he failed to sign his renunciation documents. Of course, this failure left a way open for his return to America.

The following is Snyder's account of the day Oswald visited the Embassy as typed by his secretary, and sent to the State Department.

"Throughout the interview Oswald's manner was aggressive, arrogant, and uncooperative. He appeared to be competent. He was contemptuous of any efforts by the interviewing officer to assist him, and made it clear he knew the provisions of US law on loss of citizenship and declined to have them reviewed by the interviewing officer. In short, he displayed all the airs of a new sophomore party-liner."

Second Consul McVickar wrote a memorandum in November of 1964 that stated, "it seemed that it could also have been that he (Oswald) had been taught to say things which he did not really understand. In short, it seemed to me there was a possibility that he had been in contact with others before or during his Marine Corps tour that had guided him and encouraged him in his actions." McVickar also noted that Oswald may have been following a pattern of behavior in which he had been tutored by person or persons unknown.

The above stated paragraph by McVickar is all telling in that Oswald was certainly tutored, and controlled. One would think with Allen Dulles on the Warren Commission, and him being the father of the MKULTRA program at Atsugi that just maybe this program could have been mentioned in their report. Of course this is assuming that everything the Warren Commission discussed would have been factual, and truthful.

While Oswald was staying in Minsk, he was the curiosity of the media. Seemingly, everyone wanted to interview the young Marine who wanted to denounce his American citizenship and live in Russia. Various reporters tried to interview him but few were successful. However, one reporter, Priscilla Johnson, was granted an interview.

Oswald's mother, Marguerite, was concerned about her son's safety and welfare as she had not heard from him. She was also questioned whether or not her son wanted to stay in Russia or come home. She traveled to Washington to speak with President Kennedy and when she called the Whitehouse, she was told that the President was in conference. She was then transferred to Secretary of State Dean Rusk's office where she was told that a Mr. Boster had agreed to meet with her. She met Mr. Boster who had called two more men into his office for the conference. She showed them the papers she had received and said, "Now, I know you are not going to answer me, gentlemen, but I am under the impression that my son is an agent." Do you mean a Russian agent they questioned? "No" she said, "an agent working for our government, a US agent. And I want to say this, that if he is, I don't appreciate it too much, because I am destitute and just getting over a sickness." Later, in her testimony before the Warren Commission about her meeting with Mr. Boster, Oswald's mother stated, "On January 21, 1961 was my trip to Washington. Approximately eight weeks later, on March 22, 1961, I received a letter from the State Department informing me that my son wishes to return back to the United States, just eight weeks after my trip to Washington. Now, you want to know why I think my son is an agent. And I have been telling you all along. Here is a very important thing why my son was an agent. On April 30, 1961, he marries a Russian girl approximately five weeks later. Now, why does a man who wants to come back to the United States, only five weeks later, decide to marry a Russian girl? Because I say, and I may be wrong, the US Embassy has ordered him to marry this Russian girl." General counsel Rankin bantered back and forth over why and whether Oswald married Marina for other reasons than love and told Mrs. Oswald that it was a very serious thing to say about her son and that he would do a thing like that to a girl. Oswald's mother replied, "No, sir, it is not a serious thing. I know a little about the CIA and so on, the U-2, Powers, and things that have been made public. They go through any extreme for their country. I do not think that would be serious for him to marry a Russian girl and bring her here, so he would have contact. I think that is all part of an agent's duty." When Rankin asked her if she thought her son was capable of doing that, she replied, "Yes, I think my son was an agent. I certainly do."

While in Russia, Oswald attempted suicide. Many have speculated about his state of mind and motives for this act. The attempt could have been contrived, or may have been a desperate way to get out of something that was larger than him and that he certainly did not understand. I can certainly recall my own desperate moments while under control and trying to escape manipulation. Desperate times call for desperate measures and I think that an attempt at suicide, however feeble, may have been Oswald's way to escape control. After his suicide attempt, Norman Mailer interviewed a KGB agent who said that after Oswald was released from the hospital, he visited the Embassy to talk to an American official. He spoke in a loud clear voice, as if he were speaking to instruments that might be implanted in the wall. The agent's impression of Oswald was that he was not quite right. "A normal man would never come to such an Embassy and say, 'Okay, I will give my secrets to the Russians.' What for? What is to be achieved by such declarations? After this, no KGB man could accept his information. Is it not serious enough to risk discrediting our Soviet authorities? Whatever is given to the KGB must be done secretly, deeply, and with very strong precautions. They would never take a person who tried to commit suicide and wanted to defect. This is an abnormality." If Oswald's suicide attempt was superficial, as the KGB would have been able to ascertain from medical reports, then other suspicions would follow. Had Oswald been given an unorthodox agenda by American intelligence? Had he been dispatched to the Soviet Union as a man programmed to appear irresponsible? The KGB agent remarked, "These were questions we had to pose to ourselves, because improbable as were his actions, nonetheless American intelligence could have sent him over as a probe, a monitor, to see how we would react to such a curious stimulus. It was an improbable hypothesis but not to be entirely discarded. Oswald might be something new under the sun. After this incident, Oswald was placed in a bell jar. His actions were studied, and the KGB knew their own kind of frustration. Either Oswald was sincere, or he was skillful enough to pretend to be sincere."

The House Select Committee on Assassinations (HSCA) would later say of Oswald, "His return to the United States publicly testified to the utter failure of what had been the most important act of his life." This statement may have been true if Oswald had not been a programmed agent for the CIA. A few CIA analysts believed the suicide had been stage-managed by Moscow Center because it would have been impossible for him to bring it off all by himself. My guess is that two people in the CIA knew this was not true, Allen Dulles, and James Angleton.

Oswald traveled back to the US with his wife Marina, and their daughter. They arrived in the Fort Worth area where his mother and brother lived. He began to network with the local Russian community and became friends with George De Mohrenschildt. This has been seen as a very suspicious relationship. De Mohrenschildt, who was more than twice Oswald's age, was born in Mozyr, Byelorussia. He has been described as a well-educated man, tall, handsome, and quite powerful. One wonders what the two men could have had in common. However, it is believed that De Mohrenschildt may have had connections to the CIA. In 1963, prior to the assassination of President Kennedy, De Mohrenschildt was given a $300,000 line of credit by Prescott Bush's banking firm Brown Brothers & Harriman. It is interesting to note that Prescott Bush was the father of former U.S. President George H. W. Bush, who was a former director of the CIA, and the grandfather of President George W. Bush.

It is peculiar that De Mohrenschildt would befriend the "unadjusted radical" Oswald, for he was an extremely well-educated man and counted some of the wealthiest people in the world as his friends. In 1964, De Mohrenschildt defended the friendship and said, "Well, I always spoke of his straightforward and relaxing personality, of his honesty or his desire to be liked and appreciated. And I believe it is a privilege of an older age man not to give a damn what others think of you. I choose my friends just because they appeal to me, and Lee did."

Despite this positive portrayal of their friendship, in 1971, when he testified before the Warren Commission after the assassination, De Mohrenschildt was asked what he thought of Oswald. He replied that it was not pleasant to have known the possible assassin of the President of the United States. When told that Marina Oswald had looked upon him as one of their only friends, he replied, "We were not

> friends, nothing. We just were to busy to be with them, period. They were very miserable, lost, penniless, mixed up. So as much as they both annoyed me, I did not show it to them because it is like insulting a beggar, you see what I mean? I did not take them seriously at all." He continued, "Oswald was not sophisticated, you see. He was a semi educated hillbilly, all his opinions were crude. Oswald's mind was of a man with exceedingly poor background, who read rather advanced books, and did not even understand the words in them. So how can you take seriously a person like that? You just laugh at him, but there was always an element of pity I had, and my wife had, for him. We realized that he was sort of a forlorn individual, groping for something. I was not interested in listening to him because it was nothing, it was zero. After we found out what was going on in that town of Minsk, what was the situation, what were the food prices, how they dressed, how they spent their evenings, which are things interesting to us, our interest waned. The rest of the time, the few times we saw Lee Oswald and Marina afterwards, was purely to give a gift or to take them to a party, because we thought they were dying of boredom, you see, which Marina was."

De Mohrenschildt revealed under testimony that he found Marina not particularly pretty and thought she was a lost soul living in the slums with a rather unhealthy baby. He said she was the type of girl that was negligent and a very poor mother. He found this particularly amazing as she was a pharmacist in Russia. When one considers De Mohrenschildt's personality profile, it is clear that he was not the type of individual who would have dedicated a great deal of time to help Oswald. In light of the information that he gave to the Warren Commission, it appears that he did not think highly of Oswald and it is curious as to why he would have helped him at all. Perhaps the CIA was paying him for these services? Although the Warren Commission could find no evidence of subversive activities, it was believed that De Mohrenschildt had ties with the intelligence communities of several countries. In addition to making contact with Oswald in Fort Worth, he also assisted with his connections in Dallas. I find it curious that De Mohrenschildt's opinion of the Oswald's changed so drastically from positive to negative in just thirteen years.

On the day that he was to give testimony to a representative of the HSCA, he was found dead with a hole in his head from an apparent self-inflicted gunshot wound. Because his suicide occurred on the day he was to have given testimony, it was assumed that he had been murdered. However, if the assassination was not a conspiracy, why would he have been murdered? It has been said that Oswald's mother committed the murder because he spoke poorly of her son but I doubt that this was the case.

Both Oswald and De Mohrenschildt completed manuscripts. Oswald's effort was a 50 page work written in longhand. The De Mohrenschildt manuscript was titled "I'm a patsy" and was given to the HSCA by his wife Jeanne after his supposed suicide.

At one point in their marriage, the couple had a dispute and Oswald was known to have checked into the Dallas

YMCA. I am certain that during this time, the MKULTRA once again gained control of him. I am also certain that a George Alexandrovich Bouhe, along with de Mohrenschildt, were Oswald's controllers. Bouhe was born in Russia and immigrated to the US in 1924. He became an American citizen in 1939 and worked most of his life as an accountant. He was also considered the leader of a Russian group in the Dallas and Fort Worth areas. Bouhe met Oswald at a dinner party and came to help him and his family. The author Norman Mailer has stated that he thought that Oswald may have been homosexual and in a relationship with Bouhe, but I disagree with his assessment. I believe Mailer's comments to be mere innuendo and disinformation.

In addition to befriending Oswald in Fort Worth, de Mohrenschildt also assisted him in Dallas. He secured a room for him at the home of Ruth Paine who helped Oswald acquire his job at the School Book Depository. And, as previously mentioned, Kennedy's processional parade route was rerouted at the last minute to pass by this building. I am suspicious of these numerous coincidences as without assistance from others, Oswald could not have been impli-cated in the crime of the century; nothing by chance.

As much as I would like to avoid writing about Dealey Plaza, it is necessary to mention another situation in order to illustrate the control which Oswald was under. Just prior to the arrival of the Kennedy procession past the Depository, he was spotted in the building's lunch area. At that same time, witnesses had testified they had seen two people in the window of the sixth floor of the building. Not much has been mentioned about Oswald not leaving the building to watch the President's motorcade pass by. Oswald was an ex-Marine who had defected to the Soviet Union, supposedly de-nounced his citizenship, and handed out leaflets for the Fair Play for Cuba committee. Yet it is curious that as an angry political defector, he did not show enough interest to step out the door of the Depository to view Kennedy's motorcade.

Less than two minutes after the assassination the Depository was swarming with police. One officer ran up to Oswald and confronted him as he calmly drank a Coke in the lounge area where he had been seen just moments before the assassination. Obviously not knowing what had happened, he is calm and composed. Carolyn Arnold, another employee, testified that she had gone into the second floor lunch room at about 12:15 p.m. or slightly later and had seen Oswald sitting in one of the booths eating his lunch alone. Dallas Police Department Officer Marrion Baker, who was accompanied by Roy S. Truly, superintendent of the Depository, confronted Oswald in the lunch room just moments after the assassination. Truly told Baker that Oswald worked in the building, after which Baker left and continued to search for the assassins.

The following is the testimony of Marrion L. Baker given at The Warren Commission Hearings.

Representative Boggs: Were you suspicious of this man?

Mr. Baker: *No, sir; I wasn't.*

Representative Boggs: And he came up to you, did he say anything to you?

Mr. Baker: *Let me start over. I assumed that I was suspicious of everybody because I had my pistol out.*

Representative Boggs: Right.

Mr. Baker: *And as soon as I saw him, I caught a glimpse of him and I ran over there and opened that door and hollered at him.*

Representative Boggs: Right.

Mr. Dulles: He had not seen you up to that point probably?

Mr. Baker: *I don't know whether he had or not.*

Representative Boggs: He came up to you?

Mr. Baker: *Yes, sir; and when I hollered at him he turned around and walked back to me.*

Representative Boggs: Right close to you?

Mr. Baker: *And we were right here at this position 24, right here in this doorway.*

Representative Boggs: Right. What did you say to him?

Mr. Baker: *I didn't get anything out of him. Mr. Truly had come up to my side here, and I turned to Mr. Truly and I says, "Do you know this man, does he work here?" And he said yes, and I turned immediately and went on out up the stairs.*

Mr. Belin: Then you continued up the stairway?

Representative Boggs: Let me ask one other question. You later, when you recognized this man as Lee Oswald, is that right, saw pictures of him?

Mr. Baker: *Yes, sir. I had occasion to see him in the homicide office later that evening after we got through with Parkland Hospital and then Love Field and we went back to the City Hall and I went up there and made this affidavit.*

Representative Boggs: After he had been arrested?

Mr. Baker: *Yes, sir.*

Mr. Dulles: Could you tell us anything more about his appearance, what he was doing, get an impression of the man at all? Did he seem to be hurrying, anything of that kind?

Mr. Baker: *Evidently he was hurrying because at this point here, I was running, and I ran on over here to this door.*

Mr. Belin: What door number on that?

Mr. Baker: *This would be 23.*

Mr. Belin: All right.

Mr. Baker: *And at that position there he was already down here some 20 feet away from me.*

Representative Boggs: When you saw him, was he out of breath, did he appear to have been running or what?

Mr. Baker: It *didn't appear that to me. He appeared normal you know.*

Representative Boggs: Was he calm and collected?

Mr. Baker: *Yes, sir. He never did say a word or nothing. In fact, he didn't change his expression one bit.*

Mr. Belin: Did he flinch in anyway when you put the gun up in his face?

Mr. Baker: *No, sir.*

Mr. Dulles: There is no testimony that he put the gun up in his face.

Mr. Baker: *I had my gun talking to him like this.*

Mr. Dulles: Yes.

Mr. Belin: How close was your gun to him if it wasn't the face whatever part of the body it was?

Mr. Baker: *About as far from me to you.*

Mr. Belin: That would be about how far?

Mr. Baker: *Approximately 3 feet.*

Mr. Belin: Did you notice, did he say anything or was there any expression after Mr. Truly said he worked here?

Mr. Baker: *At that time I never did look back toward him. After he says, "Yes, he works here," I turned immediately and run on up, I halfway turned then when I was talking to Mr. Truly.*

The timeline and Oswald's demeanor are most interesting. It is very interesting that Oswald obviously views the surroundings and witnesses the mayhem but is not concerned. He casually leaves work and gets on a bus to travel back to his apartment where he picks up his jacket. According to his landlord, while Oswald is in the apartment a police car drives up and blows its horn twice as though it is a signal, and Oswald leaves. He then goes to the Texas Theatre and remains in the theater to watch a movie; exactly what he is controlled to do. A few blocks from the theatre, Officer J.D. Tippit is gunned down gangland style by a man who, according to eyewitnesses, does not resemble Oswald. This individual (Oswald's doppelganger) acts and walks peculiar to bring attention to himself while progressing toward the Texas Theatre. This doppelganger passed by the ticket booth without paying which brought about further attention and entered the theatre and disappeared. Who is left in the Texas Theatre? It is "Oswald the Patsy" programmed to be just where he is supposed to be. It has always puzzled me why a man who passed through a ticket booth without paying would bring the Dallas Police Department there so swiftly if you consider that just few miles away the President had just been shot. Oswald maintained he was a patsy, which is exactly what he was.

Analysis

Lee Harvey Oswald, an average young high school student wanted to follow in his older brothers' footsteps. Too young to enlist on his own, he asked his mother to sign enlistment papers that granted him the privilege to serve in the United States Marine Corps. He entered the Corps and was stationed at NAS Atsugi. He worked in the radar control tower tracking the top-secret U-2 spy plane during its flights over China and Russia. He was then unknowingly placed in another top-secret program; the MKULTRA mind control section of the CIA. It is within this program that he was molded, groomed, and brainwashed to be a courier, spy, and patsy. Oswald was granted an early hardship discharge so that he could return home to take care of his dependent mother, but instead, the CIA sent him on a mission to Russia. Oswald completed his Russian mission and gained attention by attempting to denounce his citizenship. He is accused of passing top-secret information to the Russian government that enabled them to shoot down the U-2 spy plane. He returned home with government assistance and became involved in the New Orleans chapter of the Fair Play for Cuba Committee. Because of his involvement, the CIA added additional disinformation to his character legend. He is then transferred to Dallas where he associated with the city's Russian community. He takes a job with the Coffee Company, a front for the CIA, quits, and is then placed in the Texas School Book Depository. Kennedy's parade route was changed to travel past the Depository where Oswald was required to be as a result of mind control. He was instructed to remain in the company lunch room where he casually drank a Coke. After Kennedy was assassinated in a bloody crossfire, Oswald left the Depository, and went home. While he was there, a Dallas police car approached his apartment, stopped, and signaled by honking its horn twice, after which Oswald left. We are repeatedly asked to believe that in this hectic situation, he decided to go to a movie. En route to the theater, he is confronted by a police officer, J. D. Tippit, who he decides to shoot and kill. Obviously, this act drew attention and he continued on to the theater, a dead end location, where he was instructed to wait. Police surround the theater and capture, strike, and subdue this desperate killer. Oswald is hauled off to the police department where he is accused of not only killing officer J. D. Tippit, but President John F. Kennedy. Oswald is stunned and amazed and insisted that he was a patsy. He is held without representation, even after his insistent request to receive counsel. All investigation records and testimony of what he may have said while in custody were destroyed. Jack Ruby, who knew Oswald, just happened to be able to enter the secured police station at the moment Oswald was transported to a more secure location. At that moment, Ruby shot and killed Oswald. From that time until now, and with vast amounts of evidence contrary to the Warren Commission's findings, the MKULTRA's controlled and programmed Oswald is still considered to be the alleged assassin of President John F. Kennedy.

Chapter Ten

The Honorable Men of the Warren Commission

In May 1976 the Senate Intelligence Committee voted to recommend a Congressional investigation into the assassination of President John F. Kennedy.

Most people are unaware that the United States Government House Select Committee on Assassinations (HSCA) concluded than Lee Harvey Oswald was not a lone assassin, but part of a conspiracy. If armed with this information, why hasn't the CIA or FBI diligently searched over the past 45 years, to further investigate and bring to justice these killers? Do they already know something they are not telling us in regards to the identity of the conspirators?

Currently, and on an almost a daily basis, we hear of the investigation into the murder of Jon Benet Ramsey, the young girl who was found dead in the basement of her family's home in Boulder, CO. We hear of minute tidbits of evidence that are used to solve this ten year old case. Despite the age of the case, the investigation continues and recently, a suspect was apprehended in Bangkok, Thailand. Although the suspect was found not to be guilty, a great deal of effort and time has been dedicated to this investigation. Why was the Kennedy assassination investigation discontinued?

With the HSCA's consensus that Oswald was not a lone assassin, why isn't there a group within the Dallas Police Department, the CIA, or the FBI that diligently works to solve the Kennedy assassination mystery; perhaps the most significant U.S. crime of the last century. Where is the Simon Wiesenthal, the infamous Nazi hunter, of the intelligence community when we need him? The government agencies that should be working to solve this case remain mute on this issue. It appears that the only people trying to solve this case are individual researchers who are ridiculed and maligned by these agencies who name them "goof-ball conspiracy theorists".

In regards to The Warren Commission, the most brilliant point was not in the conclusions it rendered, but in the selection of the men chosen to be its members. New Orleans District Attorney Jim Garrison, author of *On the Trail of Assassins*, stated in an interview with Playboy Magazine that, "It's impossible for anyone possessed of reasonable objectivity and a fair degree of intelligence to read those 26 volumes and not reach the conclusion that the Warren Commission was wrong in every one of its major conclusions pertaining to the assassination. For me, that was the end of innocence". Garrison also stated, "No, you don't need any explanation more sinister than incompetence to account for the Warren Report. Though I didn't know it at the time, the Commission simply didn't have all the facts, and many of those they had were fraudulent, as I've pointed out— thanks to the evidence withheld and manufactured by the CIA. If you add to this the fact that most of the Commission members had already presumed Oswald's guilt and were merely looking for facts to confirm it--and in the process tranquilize the American public--you'll realize why the Commission was such a dismal failure. But in the final analysis, it doesn't make a damn bit of difference whether the Commission members were sincere patriots or mountebanks: the question is whether Lee Oswald killed the President alone and unaided: if the evidence doesn't support the conclusion—and it doesn't---a thousand honorable men sitting shoulder to shoulder along the banks of the Potomac won't change the facts."

I have long pondered if Oswald was the lone-nut assassin the Warren Commission portrayed him to be. If so, there would obviously be no need for a conspiracy or cover-up. And, if this is the case, why maintain the secrecy of the records hidden in the National Archives, many of which have not been released even after the passing of the Freedom of Information Act? Some of the records were released with portions blacked out. The reason given for the hidden text was that it was in the interest of national security. After so many years following the assassination, how could this be so?

Some of the following quotes and statements are copied verbatim from the foreword in the Warren Commission Report.

President Lyndon B. Johnson, by Executive Order 0.1130 dated November 29, 1963, created this Commission to investigate the assassination, of John Fitzgerald Kennedy, the 35th President of the United States that took place in Dallas, Texas on November 22, 1963.

President Johnson directed the Commission to evaluate all the facts and circumstances surrounding the assassination and the subsequent murder of Lee Harvey Oswald, the alleged assassin. The Commission was to report its findings and conclusions to him and the American public. Since Oswald was only the alleged assassin, the assassination of Kennedy, the shooting of Officer J.D. Tippit, and the murder of Oswald by Jack Ruby should have been treated separately until it was proved they were linked.

Immediately after the assassination, state and local officials devoted their resources to the apprehension of the assassin. Within 35 minutes of the murder of Patrolman Tippit, Oswald was arrested by the Dallas police as a suspect in that crime. Based on evidence provided by Federal, state, and local agencies, the State of Texas arraigned Oswald within 12 hours of his arrest and charged him with the assassination of President Kennedy and the murder of Dallas Patrolman J. D. Tippit.

As speculation about the existence of a foreign or domestic conspiracy became widespread, committees in both houses of Congress weighed the desirability of congressional hearings to discover all the facts related to the assassination.

President Johnson selected the honorable men to serve on the Commission. This is a strange because if this had been a Coup de' tat, President Johnson would have been the primary suspect and beneficiary of the takeover. By his order to establish the Commission, Johnson sought to avoid parallel investigations and to concentrate fact-finding in a body that had the broadest national mandate.

The President selected Chief Justice Earl Warren as chairman of the Commission. From the U.S. Senate, he chose Richard B. Russell, Democrat Senator from Georgia and chairman of the Senate Armed Services Committee, and John Sherman Cooper, a republican Senator from Kentucky. From the House of Representatives he named Hale Boggs, Democrat U.S. Representative from Louisiana and majority whip, and Gerald R. Ford, a republican chairman of the House Republican Conference. Also chosen were Allen W. Dulles, former Director of the Central Intelligence Agency, and John J. McCloy, former President of the International Bank for Reconstruction and Development. None of the members were qualified investigators.

Because of the growing number of rumors and theories, the Commission concluded it was necessary and in the public's interest to ensure the truth in its investigation. It was ascertained this objective could not be met by the mere acceptance of reports or analyses of Federal or State agencies. Not only were the premises and conclusions of those reports critically reassessed, but so were all assertions or rumors relating to a possible conspiracy, or the complicity of others. All theories that came to the attention of the Commission, along with the suspect Oswald, were investigated.

On December 13, 1963, Congress enacted Senate Joint Resolution 137 (Public Law 88-202) empowering the Commission to issue subpoenas requiring the testimony of witnesses and the production of evidence relating to any matter under its investigation. In addition, the resolution authorized the Commission to compel testimony from witnesses claiming the privilege against self-incrimination under the Fifth Amendment to the U.S. Constitution by providing for the grant of immunity to persons testifying under such compulsion. Let it be noted that immunity under these provisions was not granted to any witness during the Commission's investigation.

Mark Lane, attorney and author of *Rush to Judgment*, offered the Commission his services to represent the interests of Lee Harvey Oswald. The Warren Commission ignored his offer and instead selected Walter Craig, president of the American Bar Association. Out of 51 Commission sessions, Walter Craig attended only two. Lee Rankin, Chief Counsel to the Commission, stated they had no intention of appointing a lawyer to act on Oswald's behalf. Rankin also stated, "The Commission is not engaged in determining the guilt of anybody." When the Commission's conclusion was issued it stated, "Lee Harvey Oswald acted alone in the assassination of President Kennedy."

The Commission rushed through its research, as its members and most of its staff were busy individuals who had very little time to devote to this task. As important as this task was, they worked under the assumption that Oswald was the lone assassin. "Come on guys, we know Oswald is guilty, the powers that be want this verdict given; lets get to work." Hoover inundated the busy staff of lawyers with so many FBI reports it was impossible for them to handle them all. In a very short time they had to interview and check hundreds of witnesses, but seemed to conveniently overlook the most important or key people.

There has always been the lingering question of why the Commission waited six months before it questioned Jack Ruby, who was certainly a key witness. The Dallas Police Department had already closed its case against Ruby before they thought about interviewing him. It seemed as though they were not interested, even though Ruby maintained there were others involved.

According to Charles Giancana in his book *Double Cross*, Chicago Mafia mob boss Sam Giancana told him that Oswald was a CIA agent. Sam Giancana should know as he and President Kennedy slept with the same woman, Judith Exnor, who carried correspondence between them. Sam Giancana was said to be responsible for Kennedy winning the Presidential election by delivering Kennedy the state of Illinois.

I may be accused of not being reasonable in my assessment of these honorable men that served on the Warren Commission. But I do not believe that a few positive actions should erase the disgrace they rendered with their collusion and conclusion while they served as members on the Commission.

Because of their connections with the government, not one member of the Commission would have been permitted under U.S. law to serve on a jury had Oswald faced trial. Only three of the seven members heard more than 50 percent of the testimony presented. Earl Warren was present for all 93 witness testimonies, but did very little of the questioning which primarily was left to the staff counsel. Warren was chosen to add dignity to the proceedings, and was credited with the first question of the first witness, Oswald's widow Marina. His question was, "Well, Mrs. Oswald, did you have a good trip here?" Mrs. Oswald answered, "Yes, Mr. Warren, there was not much turbulence. Now can we talk about my dead husband whose guilt you have already decided, so I can go back to my usual FBI harassment?"

Allen Dulles and Gerald Ford attended 70 and 60 hearings, respectively. Allen Dulles asked 2,154 questions, and Gerald Ford asked 1,772. This is not surprising since both reported back to the CIA. My presumption would be that for all the sessions or hearings, at least Ford, McCloy, or Dulles was in attendance to protect the CIA's interests. John Sherman Cooper was in attendance for 50 hearings, John McCloy present for 35, Hale Boggs 20, and Richard Russell for the grand total of 6 hearings. Of course, why attend all sessions, when the forgone conclusion was to prove that Oswald was guilty of the assassination. Other than for appearance's sake, it was really not necessary to attend any sessions.

What seems to run long and deep in this matter is the Nixon, Rockefeller, Mafia, and CIA connections. J. Lee Rankin, Warren Commission chief counsel was quoted as saying, "We do have a dirty rumor [Oswald was an FBI informant] that is very bad for the Commission.... and it is very damaging to the agencies that are involved in it, and it must be wiped out insofar it is possible to do so by this Commission." Why would the Commission deem it necessary to wipe out this dirty little rumor that seemed germane in obtaining the truth?

In a Rolling Stone magazine interview, Burt W. Griffin, a Warren Commission co-counsel was quoted as saying, "I don't think some agencies were candid with us. I never thought the Dallas police were telling us the entire truth. Neither was the FBI." And an Associated Press (AP) dispatch stated, "Washington, D.C... An agent [James Hosty] who investigated the assassination of President Kennedy testified today that he flushed down the drain a note that Lee Harvey Oswald had delivered to the Dallas office of the Federal Bureau of Investigation."

Victor Marchetti, former Executive Assistant to the Deputy Director of the CIA, delivered the following quote to True Magazine. "The more I have learned, the more concerned I have become that the government was involved in the assassination of President John F. Kennedy."

According to Spotlight magazine, Kennedy's widow Jacquelyn was the closest person to Kennedy when he was shot and she was not asked one question about her husband's injuries. Spotlight also stated that the findings of the Warren Commission were false. "The Warren Commission is itself the greatest cover-up of the Kennedy assassination. This is the major clue pointing toward the assassins of President John Fitzgerald Kennedy."

Author Harold Weisberg summarized the Warren Commission best through the title of his book *Whitewash*.

Lyndon Baines Johnson

On November 26, 1960, the press reported that the Justice Department would give whatever aid Texas officials needed in the state's investigation regarding the Kennedy assassination. And, Texas Attorney General Waggoner Carr announced that after President Kennedy's funeral that a "court of inquiry" would be called to consider the slayings. The press went on to report that Republican Senator Everett Dirksen stated the Senate would make a full investigation of the assassination of President Kennedy. Additionally, they reported that the suggestion was first made to Congress by Representative Hale Boggs of Louisiana.

President Johnson definitely would not have wanted any involvement by the Justice Department under Attorney General Robert Kennedy's influence. He would also have been very concerned about separate investigations controlled by the Senate and Texas state officials. Therefore, Johnson preempted such possible investigations and named a special commission that would submit a report directly to him – the recipient of a possible coup. J. Edgar Hoover explained how he had influenced the editors of the Washington Post to kill an editorial that called for a presidential commission. Hoover told the Post that a full report would be made by either President Johnson or some distinguished jurist. Consequently, we can see that Johnson had conversations with Hoover about naming a special commission that included a distinguished jurist. Johnson created the Warren Commission to evaluate all facts and circumstances that surrounded Kennedy's assassination and the subsequent killing of Oswald, and to report its findings and conclusions to him. All of these actions took place in less than one week after his infamous wink at Congressman Albert Thomas while he stood next to President Kenney's grieving widow and was sworn in as the 36th President of the United States. Johnson had already decided who should be the representatives on the Warren Commission. This hasty decision was necessary, and no doubt assisted by Allen Dulles and the intelligence community, in order to take the heat off the government and to curb the American public's conspiracy questions.

We must remind ourselves of who Lyndon Johnson really was. His 1948 election to the Senate was achieved by win of just 87 votes and earned him the ironic nickname of Landslide Lyndon. The election was widely believed to involve voting fraud and the Senate was asked to not certify him as a Senator. At this point in time, the democratic party had just adopted a civil rights platform that caused Senator Strom Thurmond to revolt and run for president against Harry Truman. Johnson was very much a liberal, the way the Democratic Party leaned at the time, and he was accepted as the Senator from Texas. Before his 1954 re-election, he had already become Senate Minority Leader when the Democrats gained control of the Senate. This achievement was a clear indication of his ability to acquire power. Johnson knew how to wield this power, especially for his personal benefit. For example, his wife, Lady Bird Johnson, was the only individual able to obtain a license for television stations in Austin, TX. In 1960, Johnson was able to get a law changed that enabled him to run for a third term in the U.S. Senate, while also running for vice president under John F. Kennedy. Therefore, if the national ticket lost, he could still be elected Senator. Johnson was re-elected although the election was once again fraught with voting irregularities.

President Johnson was also linked to several scandals and one of the most significant ones involved Robert

(Bobby) Baker, his former personal secretary. While Johnson was the Senate Majority Leader, he and Baker enjoyed a close relationship and he often called and described him as his right hand man. During his tenure as Johnson's secretary, Baker's net worth increased from $11,025 in 1954, to $2,266,865 just nine years later. Rumors circulated that he was involved in corrupt activities and it was obvious that such an enormous increase in his wealth could not have come about on his government salary. Interestingly, he had retained the services of the same commodities broker that later advised former first lady Hilary Rodham Clinton. Baker was found guilty of theft, fraud, and income tax evasion and served only 16 months out of his three year sentence.

President Johnson had also been associated with Billy Sol Estes, a Texas businessman who falsified records of assets he owned in order to obtain loans. Estes had also run a federal agricultural subsidies scam that earned him millions of dollars. Agriculture Agent Henry Marshall was sent to Texas to investigate the relationship between Estes and President Johnson and was later found dead with five bullet holes in his head. Incredibly, the local Justice of the Peace ruled his death a suicide, even after it was known that the weapon used was a bolt action rifle. No explanation was given on how it was possible that Marshall could shoot himself in the head five times with a bolt action rifle. This must have been the same source from where Arlen Spector and Gerald Ford devised their entry wound and magic dancing bullet theory. Most certainly this classic Texas justice would have grabbed the attention of anyone else that may have thought of coming forward with evidence against Estes and Johnson. Johnson certainly knew how to exercise power and fear for his benefit.

FBI Director J. Edgar Hoover was a close political friend of the President and they shared the distinct similarity of a strong dislike for Attorney General Robert Kennedy. Over the years, Hoover had gathered a vast amount of information on many individuals in Washington through wiretaps, electronic eavesdropping, files, photos, and conversations. Hoover was aware of President Kennedy's sexual transgressions and also knew that Kennedy shared a girlfriend with Chicago mob boss Sam Giancana. He also knew that Kennedy used the mob to try and kill Cuba's President, Fidel Castro. Hoover realized that when he reached the age of 70, he would be subject to mandatory retirement and that Kennedy would still be president. Because Johnson would become President if Kennedy were eliminated, he believed that he may be given an extension by an executive order from Johnson.

Johnson's immediate action upon becoming President marries well with his infamous smile and the wink on Air Force One to Congressman Albert Thomas. Within 12 hours he had removed the portrait of Kennedy from his office and replaced it with a portrait of himself. He also immediately fired Kennedy's secretary and on the day of Kennedy's funeral, ordered that Jacqueline Kennedy be moved out of the White House.

One should question why Johnson was not under severe scrutiny as a possible figure in the assassination as he was the individual next in line to inherit the presidency. We know he was capable of lying as he used a phony bombing incident in the Gulf of Tonkin to start action against North Vietnam that led to the loss of more than 50,000 American lives. On his deathbed, Johnson apparently (and ironically) confided to his mistress that he believed there may have been a conspiracy in the murder of John F. Kennedy and that Lee Harvey Oswald was not a lone assassin.

When do we start getting history correct? Christopher Columbus did not discover America, Paul Revere did not make his midnight ride, and Pluto is no longer considered a planet. These are just a few of the false historical and scientific facts we were taught. Lyndon B. Johnson does not deserve a library in his name and J. Edgar Hoover does not merit a Federal building in his honor. Let's start getting it right; Lee Harvey Oswald did not kill President John F. Kennedy.

During his presidency, did Johnson ever try to find the real assassins and correct a grievous error by his rush to judgment on The Warren Commission verdict? The answer is a resounding no. President Lyndon Johnson is considered one of the honorable men.

Earl Warren

The White House tapes revealed that President Nixon and H.R. Haldeman considered the creation of another Warren Commission to investigate Watergate, complete with Chief Justice Earl Warren. Haldeman said, "But if you want Earl Warren, he'll do it…" The relationship between Nixon and Warren has often been questioned and after Warren's death, an empty folder was discovered among his effects entitled "Correspondence with Richard Nixon". Earl Warren had been manipulated by Richard Nixon.

Many have also asked why Warren accepted the position to investigate the assassination of President Kennedy. When he was first offered the position he declined; why the change of heart? He maintained that he joined the commission upon the personal request of President Johnson and his insistence that it was in the nation's interest. Another member of The Warren Commission, John McCloy, stated that he heard Earl Warren recount President Johnson's words, "When the country is confronted with threatening divisions and suspicions and its foundation is being rocked…the gravity of the situation is such that it might lead to war; and if so, it might be a nuclear war… the first nuclear strike against us might cause the loss of 40 million people." According to McCloy Warren responded, "Mr. President. If the situation is that serious, my personal views do not count. I will do it."

One of the most important events that illustrates Warren's character is how he treated the Japanese population when he was attorney general for the state of California. During his tenure, he supported the internment of Japanese and Americans of Japanese descent during Word War II. I believe the course of action Earl Warren took against the Japanese population was most surprising as he was born of Norwegian immigrants. The following was written by Mark Weber and appeared in the Journal of Historical Review. He writes, "Perhaps the most surprising advocate of evacuation was Earl Warren. Considering his later career as a vociferous liberal, it is at least ironic that, more than any other person, Warren led the popular sentiment to uproot and incarcerate the Japanese. As Attorney General of California, Warren cultivated popular racist feeling in an apparent effort to further his political career. He was an outstanding member of the xenophobia "Native Sons of the Golden West," an organization dedicated to keeping California as it has always been and God Himself intended it shall always be "the White Man's Paradise" The "Native Sons" worked "to save California from the yellow Jap peaceful invaders and their White-Jap co-conspirators."

In February 1942, Warren testified before a special Congressional committee on the Japanese question. He planned to run for California governor that year and would be elected to that position. Warren falsely testified that the Japanese had infiltrated themselves into every strategic spot in the state's coastal and valley counties. In one of the most amazing feats of logic ever performed by a lawyer, Warren claimed that the very fact that no Japanese had so far committed any disloyal act was proof that they intended to do so in the future! Warren used this type of logic throughout The Warren Commission's proceedings to judge the guilt of Lee Harvey Oswald.

Later, when the government began to release Japanese whose loyalty was above suspicion, Warren protested that every citizen so released had to be kept out of California as a potential saboteur. With comments like this, Warren played to popular racism to further his political career. It is ironic that later as Chief Justice of the Supreme Court, he presided over the exceptionally liberal "Warren Court" which ushered in an era of racial equality and unprecedented racial chaos that followed the 1954 Brown v. Board of Education decision that overthrew segregation in public schools.

As head of The Warren Commission, he sat in judgment of Lee Harvey Oswald's. This is just one more example of a fair, just, and honorable man.

Richard B. Russell

Richard Russell was born in Winder, GA, and earned his law degree from the University Of Georgia School Of Law in 1915. Russell never married and was known to carry extreme right-wing views. He was elected Governor of Georgia at age 33 and served as that state's senator. Russell was also Chairman of the Senate Armed Service Committee and in this capacity he established a relationship with the directors of the CIA. Senator Russell was not part of the Eastern establishment and was a Dixiecrat and segregationist who opposed President Kennedy's civil rights and military programs. As a Southern Senate leader he had repeatedly blocked and defeated civil rights legislation. He co-authored the Southern Manifesto and had developed the reputation of being the leader of the white supremacists in the Senate. In the face of this information, would you consider him a fair and reasonable man? And, if you were of a minority race, would you want to sit in his judgment?

Russell was also a mentor of Lyndon Johnson and had promoted Johnson's Senate career. He spent many weekends with the Johnson family and Johnson's daughters affection-ately referred to him as "Uncle Dick" - - which may be an absolutely correct description.

Russell attended only six of the fifty-one sessions held by the Warren Commission and was the only dissenting member. He was known to carry extreme right-wing views and it seems that this may have contributed to his being unable to be influenced by those members on the Commission with an agenda. He held onto his belief that the Cubans and Russians were responsible for Kennedy's assassination. This position must have pleased Allen Dulles, John McCoy, Gerald Ford, Nelson Rockefeller, and Richard Nixon. They must have felt that there was no danger in letting Russell run off on a different course just so long as he did not reveal the truth. Russell's dissent benefited the Commission as it underscored that its conduct was legitimate as there was a difference of opinion. Nonetheless, how did Russell move from this difference of opinion to sign the final Commission report that stated that Oswald was a lone assassin?

Interestingly, Russell had maintained throughout the investigation that there had been a conspiracy, and that Oswald had not acted alone. He refused to sign the Warren Commission report until a clause was added that stated that the Commission's conclusions represented a judgment based on "the best information available" (which, of course, was completely false). By demanding this inclusion, he recognized that something was amiss and as a good politician, he was not going to be hung out to dry. He also had a difficult time accepting the Magic Bullet Theory that suggested that a single bullet passed through President Kenney's neck, hopped, skipped, and jumped to pass through Governor Connally's chest and wrist to finally rest in the Governor's thigh. Lyndon Johnson's response to Russell's doubt was, "Well what difference does it make which bullet got Connally?"

Because Russell was an avowed white supremacist, I have a difficult time accepting that he was not only a United State Senator, but was selected to be a member of The Warren Commission. I am certain it was because he was just another honorable man.

John Sherman Cooper

John Sherman Cooper graduated from Yale University and was a member of its secret Skull and Bones society. After his graduation, he attended Harvard Law School but dropped out because the family's finances had been wiped out in the 1920 depression. He was first elected as Kentucky State Senator in 1946 and was elected two additional times to fill unexpired terms. During his tenure as a Senator, he was chosen to serve on The Warren Commission. Cooper worked with fellow Commission member John McCloy to help reorganize the Bavarian Judicial System in West Germany after the war and was later appointed as Ambassador to India by President Nixon.

This should indicate that an individual's appointment to The Warren Commission, regardless of the quality of service to American citizens, was beneficial to their personal career.

Fourteen years after the Commission's report, controversy erupted regarding the truth of the Commission's conclusions. A new investigation ensued and Cooper was asked to deliver testimony under oath. The following is an excerpt of Cooper's testimony.

"If you don't mind, may I make just a short preliminary statement? First, I do want to thank the chairman and members of the committee for inviting the remaining members of the Warren Commission to be here. I think it has important new questions which have caused you to conduct this investigation. I would like to say that I agree wholeheartedly with the statement made by President Ford. We conducted our investigation, in the way he explained. I don't know whether you will go into that question with me, but we were not pressured in any way by any person or by any organization. We made our own decisions, as the President had asked us to do, and as we determined to do on the basis of what we thought was right and objective. We knew each other. I had known every member of the commission before in some way. I cannot say we were intimate friends but we did know each other. These views of our work, our responsibilities and judgments happened 14 years before this date. Also, I appreciate the facts that recent studies and events in the intelligence community have raised."

There are no new facts, just more exposure of the existing cover-up. Cooper obviously knew about the problems that originated within the Commission and the problems with its conclusions. He indicated this at the end of his testimony and asked if he could speak on one particular question he had been asked during his testimony. He asked if it would be permissible for him to make two or three comments.

"First, I would like you to consider the difference in the time from 1963 to date. The FBI, at that time, was headed by Mr. Hoover who had been appointed Director continuously. He had I would say, a good reputation. I don't think anybody ever thought about the CIA meddling in internal affairs. The shock of the president's death called for an immediate investigation. It actually lay in the jurisdiction of Texas. There was no law that would permit the Congress to investigate. We were given that right by statute, also the right to subpoena witnesses and also to give immunity. We never gave immunity to anyone. We provided complete protection to witnesses—right of attorney, right of record, right to cross-examine, and open hearing if they desired. Only Mr. Lane asked for an open hearing. We also had adviser's sitting in with us from Texas; Mr. Jarworski, well-known today, the president of the American Bar Association; also Mr. Louis Powell, now Justice Powell of the Supreme Court, sat in at times. They took turns, and Mr. Eberstadt of New

Orleans, former president of the American Bar Association."

"Now I just want to say this. As far as the killing of the late President Kennedy, we will always remember it with sadness. There is no evidence of any kind except that is directed toward Oswald: his rifle was purchased under an assumed name, but directed to his post office box; the cartridge shells which were down on the floor; the tests which showed that this was the only rifle had the markings which were shown on the bullets; the fact that a man was seen by several witnesses, not identified, but seen in the window with the general description of what he looked like; his flight immediately; the fact that within a few minutes it was radioed that the killer perhaps came from the Texas Book Depository and radio cars were circling the city. That is the reason Tippit was circling the city; the fact Tippit was killed and his killing witnessed by several witnesses brought Oswald to the Texas police office. The police had already found the cartridges and the rifles, and the bag in the Texas School Depository and within a half an hour, those facts were known. Now people have said that somebody told them that they saw somebody on the railroad bank or saw somebody going over the bank, but no one has ever been able to show any cartridges, and rifle, and pistol, no one has ever found anything other than the evidence about Oswald. I would like that to be known; these facts are in the summary which I think is a very good one."

"The intelligence investigation under the leadership of Senator Church, which I know has helped cause this investigation by you, points out that the agencies did not disclose certain facts to us and that certain plots were going on. At the time we were in session, they should have been disclosed to us; they

were not disclosed to us. We knew nothing about
them. There was no testimony of conspiracy—
Oswald's efforts to get in touch with the Soviets
and with the Cuban Fair Play groups in New York
were rebuffed, rebuffed at every step—I think he
felt he was a failure and for the United States and
for President Kennedy and all of us. He knew he
was a failure at everything he tried, frustrated, with
a very sad life, but he was a Marxist. Very curious,
at the age of about 13 years, he began to study
Marxism and he kept on in his writing, affirming
that he was a Marxist. Probably he did want to show
himself as a great, supreme Marxist. Rather, like the
anarchists of the last century, he didn't care if he
was killed or not. They just wanted to be known.
We found no trace of any conspiracy. Our staff not
only received the reports from these agencies, they
examined them. They questioned them. They went
to the files of the FBI and CIA to see if there was
any informant, if Oswald was an informant. They
did a thorough job and I join with President Ford
and Mr. McCloy in praising them. But they did not
disclose to us all the facts. I wanted to make this
statement to make it clear that I concur wholly in
what President Ford and Mr. Mc Cloy have said that
we did our best. We found what we could at that
time—the truth. If somebody else can find something else which we didn't find, that of course, is a
duty on their part, as is the truth. It will be the truth.
I do make this final statement. I don't think many
people have ever read the report. Who has read 26
volumes of this case? How many read the summary? If you read the summary, it takes a long time.
Everything is in there and one of the reasons I know
few people have read the summary is there are some
very interesting little side stories in it, the newspa-
permen and others would have published. For example—and I will quit—the press dodge that was

put out on the streets in Dallas, in this summary, it shows that author just before he was discharged from the Army; in Munich, he and a comrade demanded to go back to Dallas; they were trying to figure out ways they could make the quickest, and they said, we will go back to Dallas we will infiltrate the John Birch and YAF and that's what they did. I just have talked too long, but I congratulate you on the efforts you are making. I am very proud to come back, to speak on the disinterested effort we have made and I believe that, with all due respect, that the decisions we made, when we turned our final report over to President Johnson, will stand in history."

Given that Senator Cooper was 14 years older when interviewed by this committee, one can certainly read his unspoken thoughts of those particular situations within the report that he thought were questionable. If they were questionable, and Cooper had made a statement that new information may be revealed that indicated this, then how could they place the final stamp of approval on the Commission's report? Was this just another decision from an honorable man?

Thomas Hale Boggs, Sr.

Hale Boggs received both his bachelor's degree from Tulane University in 1934 and his law degree in 1937. Boggs was elected to the U. S. House of Representatives in 1941 where he served until 1943. Boggs was House Majority leader and in his first year in Congress was responsible for bringing about the largest cash and land transfer to the Native Americans in the history of the United States. The transfer consisted of 44 million acres, and almost one billion dollars. This transfer and purchase was required to establish a clear title for the right-of-way for the Trans-Alaska pipeline. Since its completion, this pipeline has supplied almost 25 percent of the United States' oil needs.

According to Aaron Kohn, long time director of the New Orleans Metropolitan Criminal Commission, Boggs was supported financially by Carlos Marcello. Marcello was a New Orleans Mafia King and an outspoken enemy of both John F. Kennedy and Robert Kennedy.

As a member of the Warren Commission, Boggs did not agree with its findings and was its only dissenting member. He refused to sign its report until just before it was submitted and thought that a more through investigation should have been completed. This view, and his contemplation to have the investigation reopened, did not serve him well. On October 16, 1972, Boggs boarded a twin engine Cessna 310 along with Representative Nick Begich of Alaska. The two Congressmen, along with two accomplished pilots, disappeared on a political junket flight from Anchorage to Juneau, Alaska, and were never seen again. The most massive rescue search conducted to date involved 40 military and 100 civilian aircraft. The search was abandoned after 39 days, and because of this incident, Congress was prompted to pass a law mandating that emergency locator transmitters be installed on all public aircraft. I question why at even this late date, we cannot find the missing plane. We can, via satellite, find tombs buried thousands of years ago in the Valley of the Kings, and, oil companies are using satellites to search for oil deposits. Is it because the powers-that-be do not want to find the missing Boggs plane?

In 1992, under the Freedom of Information Act, Roll Call magazine discovered an FBI telex indicating that the Boggs plane was located but never retrieved. Information obtained by a verified government source with a military background described the location of the plane and stated there were two survivors. This information was available shortly after the plane had disappeared. The information also indicated than an undisclosed firm involved in testing advanced surveillance equipment had located the crash. According to the FBI, a telex was sent to FBI headquarters in Washington D. C. where presumably it was passed on to Acting Director L. Patrick Gray. The previous director, J. Edgar Hoover, had been in considerable conflict with Boggs and Boggs had called for Hoover's resignation on the floor of the Congress. Boggs was one of the most powerful people in the country during a time when the corruption of power was just becoming evident. The Warren Commission and the cover-up of the Kennedy assassination was just the beginning, and it continued on with the Watergate scandal and the resignation of President Nixon.

The events surrounding Boggs' disappearance have been wrought with conspiracy theories. These theories stem from his desire to reopen The Warren Commission report, his outspoken opposition of FBI Director J. E. Hoover, and that Richard Nixon may have wanted to thwart the investigation of Watergate.

Other interesting aspects surround the disappearance of Boggs. The chauffer that gave him a ride to the airport on the first leg of the fateful trip was a young Democrat by the name of William Jefferson Clinton, who later became President of the United States. It is often joked that the leading cause of death in Arkansas is knowing Bill Clinton. Both Begich and Boggs won their elections, but when Boggs was not found, there was an election for his vacant seat which his wife Lindy Boggs campaigned for and won. She held the position as Congresswoman for 18 years. Later, when Clinton was president he appointed Lindy Boggs to be ambassador to the Vatican. She also served as a board member and director of the National Archives, which is responsible for keeping hidden information regarding the Kennedy assassination.

Award-Winning journalist and author Cokie Roberts, who co-anchors the ABC News program *This Week* with Sam Donaldson, is the daughter of Hale Boggs. Roberts also served as a panelist on *This Week with David Brinkley* and was senior news analyst for National Public Radio as its congressional correspondent for more than 10 years.

Boggs' son Thomas told the press in 1975 that the FBI had leaked detrimental information to his father in regards to the personal lives of researchers who were investigating the Kennedy assassination. The Washington Star News, on January 31, 1975, ran a story that was captioned *Boggs Son Tells of Files on Warren Panel.* Thomas Boggs said his father had given him FBI dossiers on critics of The Warren Commission with the intent of discrediting them. The files were described as sex files and described left wing organizations to which they belonged. Two of the individuals mentioned were author Edward J. Epstein, and lawyer-author Mark Lane who wrote the book *Rush to Judgment.* I can understand how Mark Lane made the list, but not Epstein as he supported the Commission's conclusion and believed that Oswald was a lone assassin.

The government entered the Hale Boggs museum at Tulane University and removed most of his personal papers. After reading the questions and answers of the Warren Commission I do believe that Hale Boggs was indeed one of the Honorable men, but where did that get him?

Gerald Rudolph Ford

President Gerald R. Ford died of heart failure on December 26, 2006, at the age of 93 years. During his nearly week-long funeral he was described as just a humble man from Grand Rapids, Michigan. However, Ford was far from humble as he walked the halls of power most of his life. He was a University of Michigan graduate and later attended Yale where he received his law degree and most likely had his first contact with Yale's secret society, the Skull and Bones. Even in death I felt we viewed a Saint being eulogized as thousands of people in California, Washington, and

Michigan passed by his casket to pay their respects. Ford had helped to plan this elaborate funeral that did not seem to be the funeral of a humble man. A handful of friends and relatives in attendance would have been the request of a humble man. Forty four years ago in Dallas, TX, a young man by the name of Lee Harvey Oswald had a humble funeral. I determined that Gerald Ford would have been 50 years old when he served on the Warren Commission. This means he had lived 43 very good and favorable years since the misleading Warren Commission's report was published. Not so fortunate was the honorable Marine Manchurian Candidate and patsy Oswald, who has been moldering in his grave since 1963. Oswald's family has had to endure the shameful stigma of him being declared guilty without a trial, for his alleged assassination of President John F. Kennedy.

Ford was appointed to the Commission by President Lyndon B. Johnson. At the time, Assistant FBI Director William Sullivan stated, "Hoover was delighted when Ford was named to the Warren Commission." The director wrote in one of his internal memos that the FBI could expect Ford to "look after FBI interests - - and he did, keeping us fully advised of what was going on behind closed doors. Ford was our informant on the Warren Commission." Indeed, FBI documents disclose an intimate and clandestine relationship between Ford and the FBI and demonstrate he fed top-secret information to the Bureau while he was a member of the Warren Commission. An internal FBI memo dated December 17, 1963, detailed the items Ford passed to Cartha D. DeLoach, then the assistant to Director J. Edgar Hoover. Ford never revealed to the other six members of the Warren Commission his course of inappropriate and illegal behavior.

Gerald Ford used his pencil to change, just slightly, documentation of the entry wound placement of one of the assassination bullets on Kennedy's body. The effect of Ford's change was to bolster or fortify the commission's conclusion that a single bullet passed through President Kennedy thereby justifying that Oswald was a lone assassin.

This was a very crucial element that affixed the blame on Oswald. "This was a small change," Ford had said, "made just to clarify meaning, not to alter history. My changes had nothing to do with a conspiracy theory, but my changes were an attempt to be more precise." It has been said this was the most significant lie in the entire Warren Commission report. The effect of Ford's edit was to suggest the bullet that struck Kennedy in the neck was two or three inches higher. With this alteration the public could be bamboozled as to the true number of assassins involved. In legal terms, this is called tampering with the evidence. Gerald Ford was a former Eagle Scout and therefore knew the correct course to take while he served on the Warren Commission. He stated, "It is just that power corruption thing which tends to get in the way of taking the honorable correct action." Ford must have experienced great guilt as he later co-authored the book *Portrait of the Assassin* that attempted to bolster his position in the cover-up of the conspiracy and any possible culpability in the assassination coup of President Kennedy.

Without Ford's adjustment to the entry wounds record, Arlen Specter's single bullet theory would not have stood up under close scrutiny; which it still does not. Both President Ford and Senator Specter certainly did not suffer politically by these enormous gaffes. I recently read that Senator Specter is ranked as the second most powerful senator in the US Senate. This is a remarkable position to hold after he authored one of the biggest lies or mistakes of the Twentieth Century. Many years ago, in an article printed in the Chicago Tribune, the late Mike Royko stated that he thought that the members of Congress and the Senate should be addressed not as honorable or distinguished gentleman from whatever region their origin, but would the womanizer, drunkard, or scoundrel from that region please standup. There should be more truth.

The Warren Commission concluded that a single bullet fired by a discontented Oswald passed through Kennedy and another passenger Governor John Connally. A second bullet supposedly fired by Oswald from the Texas School Book Depository fatally ripped through President Kennedy's head killing him instantly. Without this single bullet justification or theory there would have had to been a second assassin thus Lee Harvey Oswald could not have been the Lone Nut Assassin. This could lead investigators to the true assassin's which would have prevented the "coup de' tat."

Gerald Ford was the only unelected president of the United States, having been appointed by President Richard M. Nixon. Ford later pardoned President Nixon who resigned under a cloud of misdeeds and controversy while in office. This pardoning action was supposedly done to help heal the nation, and to spare the nation from months of turmoil, and anguish. The constitutional amendment which allowed President Nixon to appoint Gerald Ford Vice President of the United States was approved by the Senate on September 29, 1964, less than twenty four hours after the Warren Commission Report was published. It is strange how everything is always a mere coincidence.

I respond that Ford sold his soul to the Warren Commission and he could now be coerced and used advantageously by the people in power. The quest for power does have its price.

Gerald Ford was later appointed Vice President by President Richard M. Nixon. To a politician, power is an uncontrollable aphrodisiac. When President Ford appointed Nelson E. Rockefeller as Vice President the country now had an unelected vice president, appointed by an unelected president who had been appointed by a president who later resigned the presidency in shame only to be pardoned by the vice president he had appointed. This maneuver certainly has all of the markings of a political coup de' tat.

While president, Ford tried to reorganize the intelligence community and tightened government secrecy and incorporated penalties for officials who divulged classified information. The United Press reported that documents released under the Freedom of Information Act indicated that the FBI considered Ford its spy on the Warren Commission. Interestingly, in 1974 President Ford vetoed an effort to expand the Freedom of Information Act. Playboy Magazine published an article that stated they had discovered information that Ford had allegedly received campaign funds from the CIA in 1968. President Ford appointed George Bush as director of the CIA; another Yale graduate and Skull and Bones member.

I'm sure the CIA appreciated Ford's book *Portrait* as it made only a slight reference to the charge by Oswald's mother that her son had been a CIA agent. In the July 17, 2000, issue of USA Today an article by Susan Page was printed entitled, *Looking Back, Ford Says He Has No Regrets*. In the article, Ford continued to justify his position in the bungling of facts while he served on the Warren Commission. He is quoted as saying that he, "has no doubt Lee Harvey Oswald acted alone in assassinating Kennedy." This statement was made even after the House Select Committee on Assassinations came to the opposite conclusion years earlier. In the article, Ford was quoted as saying, "I hope historians 50 years from now would say that (When) President Ford took over in a very difficult time-when we had the Watergate scandal, the war in Vietnam, economic problems-and in a period when there was great distrust of the White House, he restored public confidence." I maintain that the trust and truth was broken years before when he served as a member on the Warren Commission. As the saying goes, "that's my story, and I'm sticking to it."

Our current President George W. Bush has declared himself the Decider. I refer to Ford as the Divider, even though he looked upon himself as the Healer. The United States has yet to heal because of decisions he made as a member of the Warren Commission and for the pardon of President Richard M. Nixon.

Gerald R. Ford was the last living member of the Warren Commission, and when he died, a chapter in American History died as well.

Allen W. Dulles

My commentary on Allen Dulles will be brief as information concerning him appears frequently throughout this book. Dulles was fired prior to the assassination by President Kennedy, and was angered by the fact the President backed out of his Bay of Pigs project to invade Cuba and overthrow Fidel Castro. With this decision, President Kennedy had angered some very wealthy, powerful, and dangerous men who were not going to let him think that he was the leader and decision-maker of the country. At that time, and even more so today, the US was run by the intelligence community. Once one realizes this fact, the passionate but futile ranting of politicians becomes almost humorous as they try to correct wrongs and make positive political decisions. Dulles, along with fellow CIA men James Angelton, Richard Bissell, Richard Helms, David Atlee Phillips, and Ray Cline, controlled and orchestrated most of the pertinent information coming in and out of the Warren Commission.

Dulles is considered to be the most famous CIA director of all time. The law firm of Sullivan & Cromwell LLP, of which Dulles was a partner, represented the interests of the Rockefellers. Dulles also served as the Chairman of the Council on Foreign Relations. He was the ultimate master spy and in charge of Operation Paper Clip that relocated Nazi war criminals to South America after the war. Additionally, he was involved in the establishment of the Black Eagle Trust, a top-secret slush fund created to hold war spoils.

Dulles had an ax to grind with Kennedy and therefore, should never have requested to serve on the Warren Commission. If truth be told, he most likely appointed himself to the Commission. It is tragic that Allen Dulles is considered to belong to the ranks of honorable men.

John J McCloy

John J. McCloy graduated from Amherst College and entered Harvard Law School but his studies were interrupted by the war where he served in France with the Allied Expeditionary Force as a Captain of Field Artillery.

In 1940, Henry L. Stimson, Secretary of War, requested that McCloy come to the War Department and on April 22, 1941, he was appointed Assistant Secretary of War. Between the wars, McCloy traveled frequently in Europe and worked on litigation that enabled him to be familiar with German espionage and sabotage activities. He spent most of his time working on issues involving postwar Germany. Frequently, the question has been asked, "Is McCloy connected to the internationals?" The answer most often given is that it is more accurate to say the internationals are connected to him.

Harpers Magazine printed an article, Minister Without Portfolio, that delved into McCloy's background. The article discussed his mission in Germany in the 1920s to investigate World War I sabotage. He remained in Germany for some time where he met Adolph Hitler and became friends with some of his cohorts. McCloy was connected to Sullivan & Cromwell, a Rockefeller banking firm that kept its German investments going even after the Holocaust began. McCloy was also an official in the Office of Policy Coordination and on numerous occasions worked on CIA operations in postwar Europe. While in Germany, he blocked efforts by the Jewish community in America to act against the Nazi concentration camps. The government knew they existed, and also knew the locations of the camps. The Jewish community wanted the military to bomb the death camps or the railroads leading to them. McCloy's response and reason for inaction was that he feared repercussion. What repercussion could have been worse than what was already taking place in Germany? This is a chilling thought when you consider that during this same period, and while serving as Assistant Secretary of War, McCloy and his cohorts Earl Warren and S. Dillon Reed set up Japanese-American internment camps within the US. Against their will, Japanese-Americans were taken from their homes and imprisoned in what many refer to as "prison camps." Throughout his life, McCloy continued to speak openly against any compensation for the Japanese people that were interred, and still believed it was proper for US Government to lock them up and treat them in such a manner.

In an essay published in the *New Yorker Magazine,* author Richard Rovere reported McCloy to be the chairman, director, and president of the Establishment. He wrote of McCloy's term as High Commissioner for Germany. During this time he pardoned Alfried Krupp who was convicted of using forced labor in his steel company that outfitted the German military.

After the war, only eight war criminals were sentence to death for all of the devastation that had taken place. Another eight were given prison sentences and almost all were released within a few years, in large part due to McCloy's intervention. Ironically, in a White House ceremony hosted by President Reagan, the German government presented an award to John McCloy for his excellent work in Germany. This award is on parallel with the award that President George W. Bush bestowed on CIA Director George Tenet after the 9/11 attack on the World Trade Center. Tenet's award was given to him for his wonderful work to keep us safe from terrorists and for the great information the CIA gave the president and military regarding weapons of mass destruction. Of course, those weapons were never found and the US is now mired down in the Iraq war.

To McCloy's credit, it should be noted he was against dropping the atomic bomb on Japan. He believed we should develop peace negotiations and also forewarn the Japanese of the destructive force of the bomb to give them a chance to surrender. The following are quotes McCloy gave at a special meeting with President Truman and Henry Stimson. "We ought to have our heads examined if we don't explore some other method by which we can terminate this war than just by another conventional attack and landing." When President Truman asked what he had in mind, McCloy offered his ideas for obtaining surrender by diplomatic methods. "Some communication to the Japanese government which would spell out the terms that we would settle for— there would be surrender: I wouldn't use again the term 'unconditional surrender', but it would be a surrender that would mean that we would get all the important things that we were fighting for . . . if we could accomplish our objectives without further bloodshed, there was no reason why we shouldn't attempt to do it." His intent was to warn Japan of our military superiority, and that we would, "permit Japan to continue to exist as a nation, that we would permit them to choose their own form of government, including the retention of the Mikado, but only on the basis of a constitutional monarchy." It was during this meeting that McCloy mentioned something no one spoke of; the atomic bomb. He said, "I had raised the question whether we oughtn't to tell them that we had the bomb and that we would drop the bomb. Well, as soon as I mentioned the word "bomb" - the atomic bomb - even in that select circle . . . it was sort of a shock. You didn't mention the bomb out loud . . . Well, there was a sort of a gasp back at that." Truman told McCloy to take his ideas to the State Department for consideration. The idea was rejected and throughout his life McCloy maintained that, "we missed the opportunity of affecting a Japanese surrender, completely satisfactory to us, without the necessity of dropping the bombs." The use of nuclear weapons in Japan "was not given the thoroughness of consideration and the depth of thought that the president of the United States was entitled to have before a decision of this importance was taken." This statement shows that McCloy did know the correct course of action to take.

After the war, McCloy returned to the United States where he resumed his position as Rockefeller's attorney and engineered the merger of the Chase and Manhattan Banks. It is interesting to note that the Chase Manhattan Bank was employed by the CIA to launder funds and that McCloy was installed as a Director of the Chase Manhattan and Rockefeller Foundations. In the book *Gold Warriors,* Sterling and Peggy Seagrave write that McCloy was the original planner of the Global Black Eagle Trust that used war pillage from the Nazis and Japanese to fund covert operations. Former CIA Director Allen Dulles also oversaw this Trust and helped to set up scores of slush funds around the world. According to some sources, the Black Eagle Trust could only have been set up with the cooperation of some of the most powerful banking families in America and Europe including the Rockefellers, Harrimans, Rothschilds, Oppenheimers, and Warburgs. McCloy was also the key man in setting up the M-Fund and other political action funds. These funds remained "off the books" and some fell into the wrong hands, where they remain to this day, bigger than ever. According to reliable sources in Washington and Tokyo, in 1960, Vice President Nixon gave one of the largest of these funds, the M-Fund, to the leaders of Japan's Liberal Democratic Party (LDP) in return for their promise of kickbacks to his campaign for the American presidency. I consider this to be deeply disturbing. Then worth $35 billion, and now said to be worth more that $500 billion, the fund has been controlled ever since by LPD kingmakers who use it to buy elections, to keep Japan a one-party dictatorship, and to block any meaningful reforms. Similar abuses with other secret funds are to be found all over the world. McCloy later served as president of the World Bank from 1947 to 1949.

McCloy was a troubleshooter and expert fixer. He had stated his job was, "to be at all points of the organizational chart where the lines did not quite intersect." During the war, he made continual trips around the world solving problems and working with statesmen, bankers, and generals. He was intensely involved in backstage strategy and understood, to borrow from Cicero, "the sinew of war is unlimited money." A wheeler-dealer, McCloy knew all the ins and outs of international finance. After the war he became a name partner in the international financial services law firm of Milbank, Tweed, Hope, Hadley & McCloy, which handled the affairs of the Rockefeller family and Chase bank.

Although much of the preceding information was taken from the book *Gold Warriors*, the authors stated it was beyond the scope of their book to examine how McCloy and the others administered the Black Eagle Trust from the top down. Because so much of the documentation is still sealed, they stated they would have to be content with the evidence that has surfaced so far, and the players they know that were involved in the field.

President Johnson appointed McCloy to the Warren Commission to help pass judgment on Lee Harvey Oswald, so that no possible thought of conspiracy could rear its ugly head. He attended only 16 sessions of 51 and heard testimony from only 35 of the 94 witnesses. There was much at stake in making certain Oswald was the lone assassin.

In 1972 Nixon suggested the Justice Department appoint McCloy to be a special prosecutor in the Watergate hearings. To his credit, political savvy, or knowing that Nixon was going down, McCloy refused the assignment.

Nelson Aldrich Rockefeller

I include Nelson Rockefeller in this chapter because of his close relationship with members of the Warren Commission as well as his vast political power and his appointment as Vice President by Gerald R. Ford. I also maintain that Rockefeller, Johnson, and Ford were the direct beneficiaries of the Kennedy assassination Coup d'état and its subsequent cover-up.

The Warren Commission seemed to be dominated by establishment-type members who had ties to the Rockefeller family. Nelson Rockefeller was the grandson of John Rockefeller, Sr., the founder and chairman of Standard Oil. The Rockefellers had stock in United Fruit Company, a front for the CIA that operated in Latin America.

Nelson Rockefeller served as the Health, Education and Welfare Assistant Secretary during the Eisenhower Administration. In this capacity he was aware of the MKULTRA and MKNAOMI, the CIA's mind control programs at NAS Atsugi. Rockefeller, along with CIA Director Allen Dulles, also became a member of President Eisenhower's Operations Coordinating Board that reported to the National Security Council and was responsible for implementing security policies across several agencies.

In 1958, Rockefeller was elected Governor of New York and held that position until 1973. In the early 1970's he was a member of the President's Foreign Intelligence Advisory Board (PFIAB). Coincidently, another member of PFIAB, Texas Governor John Connelly, just happened to be riding in Kennedy's limousine when Kennedy was assassinated. In this same year, Walter J. Mahoney, New York State Senate Republican Majority Leader, charged the Kennedy Administration of dispatching Federal Agents to Albany, NY, to gather embarrassing information on Rockefeller. He accused the FBI and Treasury and Tax Departments of searching the state under the appearance of an ongoing gambling investigation. He also asserted that the investigation was run by the President's brother, Attorney General Robert Kennedy, "to embarrass a great American."

In 1975, President Ford created the Commission on CIA Activities within the United State to investigate allegations of improper CIA activities. He appointed Vice President Rockefeller as the chairman and the committee is often referred to as the "Rockefeller Commission." The Commission also investigated whether or not the CIA had been involved in the assassination of President Kennedy. Included in the investigation were E. Howard Hunt, Frank Sturgis, Lee Harvey Oswald, and Jack Ruby and their possible relationships with the CIA. The Rockefeller Commission agreed with the findings of the Warren Commission and stated that anything contrary to this was merely improbable speculation.

If we do a quick review we find that Gerald Ford worked for Rockefeller, and Nixon later appointed Ford as Vice President. When Nixon resigned and Ford became President, he appointed Rockefeller as Vice President and pardoned Nixon. In spite of what appears to be "good-old-boy" politics, we are to unconditionally believe Ford's assertion that Oswald acted alone when, in fact, it is known that he changed and fabricated evidence when he served on the Warren Commission. It is interesting to note that Ford's reason for quickly pardoning Nixon was to protect Americans and to heal a hurting nation. This had also been the reason President Johnson gave for his quick assembly of honorable men for the Warren Commission. As popular television pundits Penn and Teller say, "Bullshit." After having read this chapter, you will recognize the frequency with which the Rockefeller Commission and the CIA cross the lives of the members of The Warren Commission and you will see how many "chickens" the "fox" (Allen Dulles) watched in his CIA/Nixon/Rockefeller "henhouse".

If Rockefeller did not qualify or earn the right to be one of the honorable men, he certainly could have purchased the privilege. Indeed, money is power.

Chapter Eleven
CIA, Harvard, and Yale Connections

I have not calculated the percentage of people that served on the Warren Commission or its staff that had connections to Yale, Harvard, or the CIA. However, I estimate that it would be in the high ninetieth percentile, with some having been a member of multiple institutions. Many Harvard and Yale graduates became members of the CIA, and while they attended those prestigious schools, they became members of their secret societies. Possibly the most secret was Yale's The Order of Skull and Bones, also known as the Brotherhood of Death. Many members of this society have held powerful positions in government and in the intelligence community. As illustrated in the last Presidential election, candidates President George W. Bush and Democratic candidate and current Senator John Kerry, were both former members of Skull and Bones. This seemed to be a win-win situation for this secret society; this is troubling if you consider the powerful influence they could wield.

In February 2005, President George W. Bush named John Dimitri Negroponte as the first Director of National Intelligence. Negroponte graduated from Yale in 1960 alongside William H.T. Bush, the uncle of President George W. Bush. Also at Yale during this time was Porter J. Goss, former director of the CIA. All three men were also members of Yale's Psi Upsilon fraternity. Before his appointment, Negroponte served as Ambassador to Honduras, Ambassador to the United Nations, and most recently as Ambassador to Iraq. As Negroponte was born in London to Greek parents, he could not serve as U.S. President; however, he could perhaps wield even more power in his appointed position from behind the scenes. Negroponte has been criticized for his involvement in the covert funding of the Iran Contras and in the cover-up of human rights abuses carried out by CIA-trained operatives in Honduras. These criticisms seem to have little impact on President's Bush's decision to appoint him.

President Bush recently nominated former CIA Director Robert Gates to replace Donald Rumsfeld as Secretary of Defense. This appointment, by itself, may not seem unusual but it demonstrates that the same group of individuals appears to transfer from position to position within the government to maintain control of the highest positions. Gate's left the CIA after a 26 year career to serve on the staff of the National Security Council and later became president of Texas A&M University. Gates recently served as a member of the Iraq Study Group headed by James Baker III. These appointments seem to boast favoritism and could potentially be dangerous for our government as we have individuals duly elected to handle these important decisions.

Three generations of the Bush family were Skull and Bones members, Prescott Bush, George H. W. Bush, and President, George W. Bush. So exclusive is this secret society that only 15 members a year are chosen to become members. I recall George H. W. Bush using the catchphrase "a thousand points of light" and speaking of a "new world order". What takes place within our government when the nation waits for a group of old men in Texas, and elsewhere, to draw conclusions and make important decisions on what course of action the government should take? No matter how intelligent these men may be, and how well they served the administration, this is not how our democratic government is structured to operate.

As I write this book, James Baker III, the former Secretary of State under George H.W. Bush, heads the Iraq Study Group that will make policy recommendations regarding the war in Iraq to be submitted to President Bush. Is President Bush powerless to run the government? If he is incapable, then he should be asked to resign and the normal succession of leadership should step in to fill the vacancy. Baker was originally a Democrat but switched to the Republican Party and served as Gerald Ford's Undersecretary of Commerce and was his campaign manager in his unsuccessful bid for re-election. Baker also served as Chief of Staff in the first Reagan administration and as Secretary of Treasury in Reagan's second administration. Baker is a close personal friend and former campaign manager of George H. W. Bush who, at the time, was Reagan's Vice President. George H.W. Bush was the first director of the CIA to serve as the President of the United States.

These men and their circle of friends have been running our government in both elected and unelected capacities for years. The only years they have missed are those during the Clinton Presidency; however, Bill Clinton recently has been included in this "circle of friends" and his wife, Senator Hillary Rodham Clinton, is currently the leading Democratic candidate for president. Both Clintons are Yale graduates. Unquestionably, it is time to take back the control of our government from this network of aged men and place it back into the hands of our citizens. Baker may be an honorable man with the best of intentions, but he and his cohorts, along with those in the intelligence community, were not appointed or elected to govern forever. Even our duly elected presidents can serve for only two four-year terms. It is wonderful that they volunteer to share their vast amounts of experience, but this situation must change.

Previously, I mentioned the book *Armies of Ignorance* where William Corson writes that when he entered the presidency, James Carter stated that, "the incoming President is briefed by the Director of the CIA, so who is really in control and wields the power within the government?" I read that President Kennedy had committed suicide; I was quite surprised by this statement until I thought of the many powerful men whose toes he had stepped on. Kennedy withdrew support for the Bay of Pigs and was about to de-escalate the Vietnam War which would affect the large military complex. Kennedy and his brother, U.S. Attorney General Robert Kennedy, began to clamp down on the Mafia and organized crime that affected James (Jimmy) Hoffa, president of the powerful Teamsters Union. Kennedy also fired the powerful Allan Dulles. director of the CIA, whom President Lyndon Johnson later appointed as a member of the Warren Commission. Kennedy also made the fatal statement that he was going to split the CIA into a thousand pieces and send them to the distant winds. The major miscalculation Kennedy made was to think that he, as president, and the elected government was in control.

James J. Angleton
Yale, Harvard, and the CIA

Of all the people involved in the Kennedy assassination, James J. Angleton is at the forefront. James Jesus Moreno Angleton was born in Boise, ID, in 1917. His mother was a Mexican citizen and his father worked for the National Cash Register Company (NCR) based out of Dayton, OH. Angleton spent most of his childhood in Rome, Italy, as his father had purchased an Italian subsidiary of NCR. He attended the Malvern College boarding school in England, and received his undergraduate education at Yale University. Angleton attended Harvard Law School before joining the U. S. Army where he was recruited into the Office of Strategic Services (OSS), the precursor to the CIA.

It is quite telling that Oswald believed that Angleton had sent him on a mission to the Soviet Union, although he does not say he actually knew who had sent him. Oswald's mission was so well disguised that his wife Marina remarked that she did not know what the CIA was until she was already in America. It is said that Oswald was an Angleton "operation" and that no one else within the CIA knew of the operation other than a select few that were close to Angleton. When the House Select Committee on Assassinations (HSCA) investigated the CIA in regards to its possible connection with Kennedy's death, it was convinced that Oswald was not a part of a CIA operation. Of course that answer is predictable as Oswald was yet another layer away from those who answered the particular questions asked during the investigation. Oswald was controlled by Angleton and the MKULTRA program that supposedly never existed.

While at the CIA, Angleton's title was Associate Deputy Director of Operations for Counterintelligence or (DDOCI). Most who knew him said that he was obsessed with catching a mole he thought had penetrated the Agency. It is also thought he might have been like a "dog chasing its tail" as he was quite possibly a mole for the KGB. What better cover than to be always looking for yourself? Many of the secrets of the nuclear weapons technology program and the Manhattan Project were passed on to Russia by Angleton's friend, Donald Duart Maclean. Maclean was assisted in his escape to Russia and the KGB by the CIA's counter intelligence program via Kim Philby, a soviet spy and British counterintelligence agent. When one reads about the Manhattan Project and the espionage that occurred within the program, it makes one question how the U.S. Government could execute Ethel and Julius Rosenberg for this same crime. Were the Rosenbergs just another "Patsy" for James Angleton?

In 1964, former KGB officer Yuri Nosenko defected to the United States from Russia. Nosenko had stated that while Oswald lived in Russia, he had been his handler for the KGB. This is disconcerting because the CIA said Oswald was not of interest to the KGB and did not debrief him when he returned from Russia. Nosenko also claimed to have information regarding the Kennedy assassination and when debriefed, stated that he had been personally responsible for handling the Oswald case. He stated that the KGB had determined Oswald to be mentally unstable and thought it unnecessary to debrief him about his knowledge of the top-secret U-2 spy plane despite the fact that he had worked in the control tower while stationed at NAS Atsugi. Of course Oswald was not mentally unstable, but plainly suffered from the effects of being controlled by the MKULTRA program.

This information must have infuriated super mole Angleton who had obviously sent the mind controlled Oswald to Russia as a dangle. When the KGB was not duped, Angleton insisted the CIA had been compromised by the KGB. Nosenko was incarcerated and debriefed over a three and a half year period but it is even more conceivable that he was controlled and brainwashed until he would no longer be of any threat to the CIA.

Oswald had threatened to hand over U-2 spy plane secrets to the Russians and there has always been a question as to why the CIA showed so little interest in Oswald, both while he was in Russia and after he returned home to the United States. It was because Angleton secretly ran and controlled Oswald and the defection project. Therefore, Angleton deemed it unnecessary to open an Oswald dossier upon receipt of any significant information. It has been said that Angleton communicated with Oswald through a fellow Atsugi Marine, Gerald Patrick Hemming.

A few key people knew of Angleton's Oswald defection project but whether they were privy to the information that Oswald was being controlled by the MKULTRA program is unknown. Two former CIA employees, James and Elsie Wilcott, claimed that Oswald was an official CIA project and was not listed on the payroll or any official records. The Wilcott's were recruited as a husband and wife team and worked their first duty station in Tokyo, Japan. James Wilcott had said that shortly after Kennedy's assassination, there were rumors floating around that the CIA had been involved. He said that at first, this kind of talk disturbed him but that he never took it seriously and that later even more rumors surfaced. He stated that based upon what he had heard around the Tokyo Station he became convinced that the CIA did indeed kill President Kennedy. Rumors suggested that the assassination was either an outright headquarters project approved by Director John A. McCone, or it was a project completed outside the CIA and perhaps orchestrated under the direction of Allen Dulles and Richard Bissell.

Oswald said that he had been recruited from the military for the express purpose of becoming a double agent with a Soviet Union assignment. A correction should be added here in that Oswald was taken from the Marine Corps without his knowledge or consent, developed into a Manchurian Candidate, and programmed in Russian culture and language to be sent to the Soviet Union. Wilcott said that rumors persisted that the CIA had some special type of hold on him. Not knowing that the MKULTRA project was being carried on right in front of them, they speculated that Oswald had murdered someone or committed some other serious crime that had been discovered during a routine lie detector test. It was known that he had been sent to the "The Farm", a CIA training camp located at Camp Perry, VA, although it was believed that he was not part of the normal training venue. It was said that he may not have known that he had been there. Often, in special cases, subjects would be put to sleep, wake up in a strange place, and be told that it was some other place than "The Farm". It was thought that Oswald would know that he worked for the CIA, but would be rigidly compartmentalized from any of the normal activities and contact that a regular CIA employee would have. Wilcott said that although he knew people who worked on the Oswald project, no one would openly discuss it and that he would just overhear conversations about it.

As I previously mentioned, it has always been stated that Oswald had not been debriefed when he returned from Russia and I always find this incredulous. Wilcott maintains that upon his return from the Soviet Union in June of 1962, Oswald was brought back to either Yokosuka or Astugi, Japan, to be debriefed. It makes sense that he would be debriefed at NAS Atsugi but it would make little difference as the locations are only a few miles apart. Regardless, the question still lingers, "Was Oswald debriefed?"

James Wilcott had been a finance officer when stationed in Japan. The funds for the Oswald project had been drawn under the cryptonym CI/SIG (Special Investigation Group). The CI/SIG was a secret sub-section of the CIA and had a slush fund that gave Angleton access to an enormous amount of uncontrolled funds. Although Wilcott knew of the cryptonym, he would not have known how the money in this fund would be utilized. Elsie Wilcott agreed with her husband and stated that "right after the President was killed, people in the Tokyo station were talking openly about Oswald having gone to Russia for the CIA. Everyone was wondering how the Agency was going to be able to keep the lid on Oswald, but I guess they did." The HSCA concluded that "based on the evidence, James Wilcott's allegation was not worthy of belief." Elsie Wilcott was never asked to testify to verify her husband's story.

John Scelso testified before the HSCA that he had been appointed by Richard Helms to lead the CIA's investigation into the Kennedy assassination. Scelso was the cover name for John Whitten, whose identity was so sensitive that the CIA did not declassify it until 2002, two years after his death. Whitten was a CIA career man and desk officer who covered the Western Hemisphere which included the Mexico Branch. Although Helms had appointed Whitten to lead the investigation, Angleton ignored Helms' orders and worked on the investigation himself with the Warren Commission, the FBI, and former CIA director Allen Dulles, who was one of the Commission's members. Angleton coached CIA Director John McCone and FBI Director J. Edgar Hoover on what to say before they testified to the Warren Commission. Whitten told the HSCA that Angleton interfered with his role as the coordinator of the investigation and that it was eventually turned over to Angleton. Whitten also remarked that Angleton was talking with the FBI without proper authorization.

Throughout the remainder of his career, Angleton continued his search for the nonexistent mole. Angleton resigned on the eve of an upcoming Congressional investigation into the government's surveillance and maintenance of case files on more than 10,000 American citizens. Angleton was never called to testify before Congress, and in 1987 died of lung cancer at age 69. Angleton knew, but never revealed, the circumstances surrounding the assassination of President Kennedy.

Richard Helms
CIA

Richard Helms was not a member of the Warren Commission, but he was very instrumental in helping the Commission to draw its conclusions. Hundreds of Commission documents bear his signature and he was rewarded for his diligent work by an appointment as director of the CIA in 1966 by President Lyndon Johnson, the constructionist of the Warren Commission. In spite of this, Helms was cited for perjury by the HSCA for lying about his knowledge of Lee Harvey Oswald and the Kennedy assassination and for making unproven claims about Clay Shaw. He received a suspended two year sentence and the maximum punishable fine.

Helms experienced a relatively easy Directorship under President Johnson; however, things changed under the Nixon administration. After the Watergate incident, Helms moved the CIA away from its close contact with the Presidency when it came under more strict Congressional supervision.

In 1972, Richard Helms ordered the destruction of most MKULTRA records. This involved the destruction of more than 150 CIA-funded research projects designed to explore mind control. This was not known by the public until a few years later that such a project existed and only because the New York Times published a report that exposed the project.

Helms was awarded the National Security Medal by President Ronald Reagan in 1983.

Richard Mervin Bissell, Jr.
Yale, Skull and Bones, and CIA

Richard Bissell worked for the Ford Foundation but was persuaded to join the CIA. In 1958, Allen Dulles appointed him as the CIA's Director for Plans which controlled more than half of the agency's budget. This division later became known as the CIA's Black Operations. This division also developed the U-2 spy plane project and the MKULTRA program. Both Bissell and CIA Director Allen Dulles made contact and had conversations with the leading figures of the Mafia including Carlos Marcello, Santos Trafficante, Meyer Lansky, Johnny Roselli, and Sam Giancana. Note that Giancana shared a girlfriend, Judith Exnor, with President John F. Kennedy. Exnor served as a bag lady that carried information between the two men.

Through its counterintelligence division, the ZR/Rifle project, the CIA offered the Mafia an assassination fee of $150,000 to kill Fidel Castro. The biggest mistake President Kennedy made was not to provide air support for the Bay of Pigs invasion which was Bissell's Black project. Kennedy refused to send support and that placed him on the short list of items that got him assassinated. Because of the Bay of Pigs fiasco, Kennedy offered Bissell the position of director of a new department that would develop a new spy plane that would make the U-2 obsolete. However, Bissell chose to leave the CIA and Kennedy appointed Richard Helms as the new Director of Plans.

Everette Howard Hunt, Jr.
CIA

Everette Howard Hunt, Jr., better known as E. Howard Hunt, was a CIA agent who appeared as a conspirator in the Bay of Pigs operation as well as the Kennedy assassination. He was responsible for the break-in and attempted theft of psychiatric files on Daniel Ellsberg, the author of the

Pentagon Papers, and for the break-in of the Democratic National Committee at the Watergate office building.

Hunt had a very mysterious career. He served in the Navy, Army, Air Force, the OSS, and the CIA. In 1949, he was involved in the establishment of the first post-war CIA station in Mexico City. He was a high-ranking officer throughout his CIA career and was one of the main figures involved in the Bay of Pigs Invasion, an attempt to overthrow Castros' government in Cuba. Hunt was embittered when President Kennedy withdrew support of the invasion which he understood him to have promised. Interestingly, after the Bay of Pigs invasion, Hunt became Allen Dulles personal assistant.

Kerry Thornley, the Atsugi Marine who stated he was controlled by the MKULTRA, believed he had various conversations with Hunt, who was using the alias of Gary Kristein. These conversations consisted of plans to assassinate President Kennedy and took place while Thornley lived in New Orleans. I believe the American businessman I met in the small café in Yokohama was E. Howard Hunt and have made mention of him in the chapter entitled, *Hawk, an Atsugi Marine.*

Hunt was a prolific author of spy novels and his personal escapades would make an interesting book. Author Norman Mailer fictionalized his role in the Bay of Pigs invasion in the novel *Harlot's Ghost.* Hunt's own memoir, *American Spy: My Secret History in the CIA, Watergate, and Beyond,* was published posthumously in 2007.

David Atlee Phillips
CIA

David Atlee Phillips began his intelligence career in 1950 as a part-time CIA agent in Chile. Over his 25 year career, he rose to the rank of chief of all operations in the Western Hemisphere, primarily in Latin America and also

Mexico, Cuba, and the Dominican Republic. He was awarded the Career Intelligence Medal, a rarely given award that very few agents have received, and founded the Association of Former Intelligence Officers (AFIO); an alumni association comprised of intelligence officers from all intelligence services.

David Phillips entered on the Kennedy assassination scene when the HSCA reinvestigated the conclusion of the Warren Commission Report because of all of the questions that had surfaced. Some researchers believed that Phillips had used the alias of Maurice Bishop. Antonio Veciana, founder of the anti-Castro group Alpha 66 that received substantial funding from the CIA, testified before the HSCA that he had seen Maurice Bishop speak to Oswald, and identified him as being agent David Atlee Phillips. The researchers also believed that Phillips was directly connected to a CIA plot to kill President Kennedy. In his book *The Last Investigation*, author Gaeton Fonzi, who was also a former Federal investigator for the HSCA, accused Phillips of playing a key role in the Kennedy assassination. New Orleans District Attorney James Garrison charged that Clay Shaw was a CIA agent and had connections with Phillips through a CIA dummy corporation called Freeport Sulphur, and its subsidiary Moa Bay in Cuba.

Summary

Many people have asked me, "Hawk, don't you think that after all these years someone would have come forward and told the truth about the Kennedy assassination?" They also ask, "How could all of those people have kept a secret like that?"

My answer is compartmentalization. Not everyone knows the total story, only portions of it. I hold the intelligence community accountable for the assassination and the cover-up in the death of President John F. Kennedy. Not the total intelligence community, but certain people within the CIA, FBI, the Office of Naval Intelligence, the United States Marine Corps, President Lyndon B. Johnson, the Warren Commission, and the Dallas Police Department. The primary individuals responsible are those who operated and controlled the MKULTRA program that used Lee Harvey Oswald as its patsy. These individuals are Allen Dulles, Richard Bissell, Richard Helms, and James Angleton, and each of these men knew all of the compartments of the total story. The preceding men did not pull the trigger, but organized and were in control of the assassination and its subsequent cover-up.

My objective in writing this book is not to solve the Kennedy assassination, which will probably always remain an open chapter in American history, but to exonerate Oswald. I believe that he was not the assassin of President John F. Kennedy, but was what he claimed to be, "a patsy." The perpetuation of the lies, cover-up, and half truths must stop. My first-hand experience with Atsugi, the MKULTRA, and Oswald should substantiate the culpability of the CIA and Navy Intelligence. The intelligence community has always denied any connection to Oswald, and in this book I make the connection.

As stated in the preceding chapters, a good deal of information included in this book was gleaned from several books already published about the assassination. One can find disinformation books in the marketplace that have enough truth between their covers to make them plausible, thereby adding to the confusion. I have had the distinct advantage of having known Oswald, and to have served with him in Japan while in the United States Marine Corps. Additionally, we were both manipulated by the MKULTRA and traveled on a Chinese military mission into the mountains of Taiwan. Many a pundit and naysayer will question why I have waited so long to come forward with this information, as if the length of time I have held this information would change the truth. It will be difficult for many to change their long held beliefs about the assassination. The authors of many books that have been written about this controversy, some of which I have referred to in this text, may have to change their perspective. However, if they hold firmly to what they believe are the facts, they are no better than the Warren Commission that was unwilling to change and adhered to a predetermined conclusion.

Just as an abused child reacts, I felt embarrassed about what happened to me. Not only was I taken advantage of by my government, I felt foolish and responsible for having allowed the mind control to occur. I understand that just being in the military exposes one to become victimized in many ways. However, I certainly never imagined that I would be used as a nuclear guinea pig, hypnotized, drugged, and utilized as a mind controlled courier. I volunteered to serve in the United States Marine Corps, but for none of the preceding conditions.

Through the Warren Commission, the CIA maintained that Oswald was not connected to the intelligence community in any way. Oswald was most definitely connected, and his actions controlled by factions within the intelligence community. These groups include the United States Marine Corps, CIA, FBI, Office of Naval Intelligence, and their overseeing body, the National Security Agency. Government agencies are responsible for the people working within their parameters, so even if rogue factions existed, the cover-up belongs to all.

America's innocence died on November 22, 1963, and the truth was the victim. The assassination of President John F. Kennedy and its cover-up will be remembered as a low point in our history. Our government, as well as the news media and many people who were in a position to make a difference, all turned a blind eye on what took place.

It is currently the year 2008. I recently read that 90 percent of the people living in the world today had not been born in 1963. However, I am certain there are people still alive that are responsible for the Kennedy assassination and cover-up. Additionally, many innocent witnesses died at the hands of these people, and many more have been forced to hide in silence. It is tragic that some of the innocent are assumed guilty in the court of public opinion and some of the guilty have gone to their graves looked upon as honorable men with government buildings, libraries, airports, and streets named in their honor. A Coup de'etat of major proportions took place in Dealey Plaza on November 22, 1963, and the lies still persist. There should no longer be controversy as to whether President Kennedy was assassinated by the lone assassin Lee Harvey Oswald, but what conspiracy does exist?

Supposedly, the controversy was settled by the House Select Committee on Assassinations (HSCA) in 1979. The following is the conclusion of the HSCA report.

> The scientific evidence available to the committee indicated that it is probable that more than one person was involved in the President's murder. That fact compels acceptance, and it demands a re-examination of all that was thought to be true in the past. The committee's investigation of Oswald and Ruby showed a

variety of relationships, which may possibly have matured into an assassination conspiracy.

Neither Oswald nor Ruby turned out to be loners, as they had been painted in the 1964 investigation. Nevertheless the committee frankly acknowledged that it was unable to firmly identify the other gunmen; and the nature or extent of the conspiracy.

One must keep in mind the Congress of the United States of America declared that President John F. Kennedy was killed as the result of a conspiracy.

Throughout this book I have shown how Oswald and I were used and controlled by the CIA and its mind control program while we served as Marines in Japan. I have also explained how others had an association with a nefarious organization, the MKULTRA.

My intent has been to illustrate the life of a bright young man with a great deal of potential, who enlisted in the Marine Corps to fulfill his desire to become a Marine, just as his older brother Robert had done. At age 17, Oswald was neither a Marxist nor an assassin. His transformation took place while he was under the control and guidance of the United States Marine Corps.

Why was it necessary to remove Oswald's earned honorable discharge and change it to an undesirable discharge? This follows in line with discrediting Oswald in any way they could. His top-secret classification, which is only bestowed after rigorous personal profile research, had been removed from his military records just as my top-secret classification was removed from my records. When granted, this classification establishes an individual as an upstanding and trustworthy citizen. The removal of this classification was completed by the very government that Oswald and I served to protect. Oswald has been lying in a grave since 1963. This young patriotic and maligned Marine will go down in history as an assassin and traitor to his country and his family has experienced tremendous shame. Those responsible for the assassination will march into history as honorable men. This record should be corrected for as the American public and Oswald's family should know the truth and be able to stand proud.

Leo Janos, a writer and good friend of President Johnson, visited him at his Texas ranch shortly before the President's death. Johnson confided in Janos that he never thought Oswald acted alone and that the assassination was a conspiracy. He made reference to CIA-trained "mechanics" or trained assassins, who operated in the Caribbean under a program called Murder, Inc. These mechanics also possessed other devious specialties and were men who could remain absolutely anonymous. Janos later wrote an article about this conversation that was published in the magazine *Atlantic Monthly*.

Norman Mailer, in his book *Oswald's Tale, An American Mystery*, described his personal interviews with persons who had been friends and associates of Oswald during the time he lived in Minsk, Russia. Almost all of the persons interviewed could or would not believe that this mild mannered and kind person could have been guilty of the assassination.

I don't believe for a moment that Oswald was one of the shooters in Dealey Plaza and suggest that the possibility that another person, or perhaps several, were involved in the conspiracy. We have the shooter in the window on the sixth floor of the school book depository, the shooter behind the fence on the grassy knoll, the controlled Oswald, and his controller. How many others involved is not exactly known.

When Oswald was first confronted by a police officer in the School Book Depository he was standing in the lunchroom on the first floor casually drinking a Coke. He was not nervous, excited, or out of breath when the officer asked him to identify himself just moments after the shooting had taken place. His presence in the lunchroom meant that he would have had to hide the rifle and run down five flights of stairs to be there at that time. And, he had been seen there just moments before the assassination by a fellow employee. The fact that Oswald remained in the building and casually drank a Coke in the lunchroom instead of watching President Kennedy's motorcade pass by the School Book Depository certainly indicates he had been controlled.

Attorney and author Mark Lane wrote one of the first books that questioned the Warren Commission's conclusions. Lane later wrote the wonderful book *Plausible Denial* and as an attorney, was requested by the Liberty Lobby to defend them in a libel suit which had been filed against them by E. Howard Hunt. Liberty Lobby owned a newspaper called the *Spotlight* which had published an article written by Victor Marchetti, a former officer of the CIA. Hunt brought a defamation libel suit against Liberty Lobby and won a $650,000 judgment which would have driven the Liberty Lobby into bankruptcy. The article had accused Hunt of being present in Dallas on November 22, 1963, and of having played a part in the assassination of President Kennedy. (Hunt had been an employee of the Office of Strategic Services and the CIA for many years.) Lane won the Libel suit for the Liberty Lobby but little is ever mentioned in the news about this case and its implications. Stories and lies continue to be perpetuated and even as late as the fortieth anniversary Kennedy's death, the late Peter Jennings narrated a two hour documentary about the assassination. The broadcast stayed true to the same old Warren Commission story with no mention of the Liberty Lobby trial nor the conclusion of the HSCOA that Oswald had not acted alone and there had been a conspiracy. When the American public is asked "do you think Lee Harvey Oswald acted alone in the assassination of President Kennedy?" The answer is a resounding no!

Almost 150 years after the assassination of President Abraham Lincoln most people still believe that John Wilkes Booth acted alone when he assassinated the President. I once wrote an essay about the Lincoln assassination and in my research never came across any information to indicate there had been a conspiracy. Very few people know about the conspiracy that included John Wilkes Booth and multiple others. Four of the conspirators were hanged in public in Washington, D.C. on July 7, 1865, including Mary Surratt, the first woman ever executed by the United States.

How much time remains until we can open all of the information hidden in the archives, and not hide behind the excuse that National Security would be compromised? As the Warren Commission concluded that Oswald was a dysfunctional lone-nut assassin, how could this hidden information affect national security? As I previously stated, I am certain there are people alive today that had direct involvement in the assassination and its cover-up who should be exposed and brought to justice. I believe these people are extremely influential and still operate in high ranking government offices, and some are retired with legacies to be lost.

Having read this book, one can follow the path of control the MKULTRA maintained over Oswald. Individuals within this organization are quite possibly to blame for the sabotage of the U-2 spy plane over the Soviet Union that provided for the continuation of the Cold War. They are equally as responsible in their involvement in President Kennedy's assassination and subsequent cover-up. Various MKULTRA individuals were also involved in the Bay of Pigs invasion, and the Watergate break-in.

Over the years, the intelligence community has been responsible for the distribution of misinformation. Recently, it stated there were Weapons of Mass Destruction hidden in Iraq. This party line leaves the United States mired in a war that has cost thousands of young American lives with no end in sight. President Bush states that he will revamp the intelligence community, but unfortunately, he is not in control and the intelligence community will continue to thrive and flourish. I am not certain if it is possible to remove the fox from the hen house. It is difficult to control and correct an organization that essentially runs the American government, especially one that is not voted into control, but yet has been in power for almost 70 years. A well-known line at the end of a former popular television series, *The X-Files*, is very appropriate in this situation, "They are out there." Yes; they are out there and we should not rest until we find them. Witness what happened to President Kennedy when he threatened to break up the power of the CIA. Absolutely no one is safe from these men and their quest for power and control. William R. Corson, in his book *Armies of Ignorance*, cited a quote from President Carter. "I was so naïve when I became president that I did not know that King Hussein of Jordan was a CIA operative." The power/control problem will exist as long as the incoming president is briefed by the CIA director and his agency's personnel. In this instance, the fox tells the farmer that he will take good care of his chickens. The agency remains all-powerful and continues to grow in power as each new president enters office. I remind readers that the CIA was populated with the remainder of the Third Reich and the Nazi Party that came here after the war in Operation Paper Clip.

I do not believe for a moment that President Bush will do anything to make changes within the intelligence community. He may succeed in a few cosmetic changes, but substantial change will not take place and I am not certain he has the power to do so. President Bush acts as merely a figurehead to pacify the American public. Former CIA Director George Tenet was on duty when the September 11, 2001, (9/11) attacks took place upon the United States. The catastrophe was a result of terrorists flying planes loaded with highly explosive fuel into the World Trade Center in New York City and the Pentagon, near Washington, D.C. When Tenet first heard about the incident he remarked, "I wonder if it has anything to do with this guy taking pilot training."

This comment indicated that he had prior knowledge of suspicious individuals in training at U.S. flight schools. How was Tenet punished or reprimanded for this outrageous error in judgment? He was granted an early full government retirement pension, and was awarded the Freedom Medal by President Bush in a glorious ceremony. With the exception of a few individuals, the intelligence community was also responsible for erroneous information about Weapons of Mass Destruction that prompted the Iraq War. President Bush's excuse for the United States' engagement in the war was to spread democracy. Not to mention that Iraq sits on one of the largest oil reserves in the world.

We will never completely have the America we want. Our America is one we inherited from our forefathers, the signers of the Declaration of Independence. It is also the America that thousands of young men laid down their lives to protect. We must correct the past and expose the truth, and clean out the intelligence community and remove the scoundrels from government.

As I write this book, FBI Deputy Director William Mark Felt, Sr., revealed that he was the notorious Deep Throat who exposed Watergate secrets to Washington Post reporters Bob Woodward and Carl Bernstein. Many in the media have lambasted Felt for not releasing his information through the proper channels. At the time, Felt held the position of associate director of the FBI, second only to L. Patrick Gray who was appointed by President Nixon. Nixon controlled everything at this point and if Felt had used the appropriate channels, it would have been the same as committing suicide. Again, the fox was guarding the hen house. Felt should be viewed as a hero no matter how offended those individuals are that were involved in the Nixon administration. How the information was received is not as important as the truth he brought forth.

I am certain many people are going to be irate when they read the information contained within this book and my poor evaluation of those honorable men. Also, many people will hold onto old thoughts and concepts whether they are correct or not. They will not want to be bothered with the facts and will have already made up their minds about the assassination. However, these old ideas and theories will have to change just as the Sixth Floor Museum at Dealey Plaza will have to change as its story is incorrect because Oswald did not shoot President Kennedy from the snipers nest, although someone may have.

I would like to extend my apologies to the Oswald family for what they have had to endure since that fateful day in Dallas. Oswald was a patriot who worked diligently both knowingly and unknowingly for the United States government as a secret agent and was an honorable Marine.

Let us suppose you choose not to believe that Oswald and I were on a mission with the Chinese military in the mountains in Taiwan. You will still be left with the enormous amount of evidence I have compiled with regards to NAS Atsugi and the MKULTRA and its connection to the assassination of President John F. Kennedy.

****

Read not to contradict and confute,

not to believe and take for granted,

not to find talk and discourse,

but to weigh and consider.

Sir Francis Bacon